Dear Homeowner,

Please Take My Advice.

Sincerely,

An Architect

Dear Homeowner,

Please Take My Advice.

Sincerely,

An Architect

ESTABLISH BUDGETS, PRIORITIES,
AND GUIDELINES EARLY ON TO SAVE TIME,
MONEY, AND MAYBE EVEN YOUR MARRIAGE.

STEPHANIE A. WASCHA, AIA

For information about this title or to order other books and/or electronic media, contact the publisher:

Stephanie Ann Wascha, AIA
Wascha Studios
815 Seattle Blvd. South #135
Seattle, WA 98134
www.waschastudios.com
info@waschastudios.com

ISBNs:
    Print 978-0-9981176-0-7
    eBook 978-0-9981176-1-4

Printed in the United States of America

Cover and Interior design: 1106 Design

This book is dedicated to homeowners everywhere. The modifications you are about to make to your home can be difficult and scary, and I admire you for taking action to better the habitat in which you live. Not everyone does, or can, for that matter, and it makes all the difference in the world to your sense of inner peace. Seize this opportunity to really delve into your desires, challenge yourself to answer tough questions with thoughtful insight, and create your perfect Home Haven.

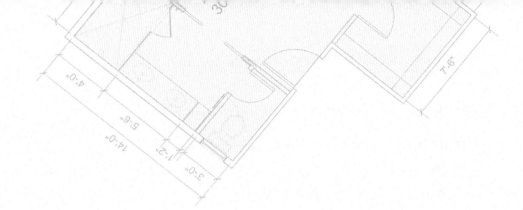

TABLE OF CONTENTS

FOREWORD

I work with homeowners to design and eventually build their ultimate treehouse on my television show *Treehouse Masters*. I help people step out of their comfort zone, think outside the box, and create something unique that their family can enjoy for decades to come. When you don't have enough information to discuss the practical aspects of your project, it is impossible to take that next creative step toward making it specific to the needs and personality of your family long term.

Stephanie Wascha's *Dear Homeowner, Please Take My Advice. Sincerely, An Architect* not only provides the necessary practical and creative guidelines to successfully get from Point A to Point B without wasting a lot of money, she also offers friendly marital do's and don'ts to make the whole process a bit smoother for you and your spouse. I work with homeowners everywhere, and I have seen firsthand the exact challenges she can help you avoid. I wish my wife and I had read this book before we did our own remodel!

Additionally, Stephanie delivers this litany of information in a slightly humorous way, making it both entertaining and informative. It is an easy, must-read for anyone looking to modify or build a home.

—Pete Nelson of *Nelson Treehouse and Supply* and host of Animal Planet's hit TV show *Treehouse Masters*

ACKNOWLEDGMENTS

Everyone needs a little help sometimes. Whether it's deliberating ideas, proofreading, discussing the use of various strange words, getting legal advice, or good old fashioned emotional support, we have our gold medalists! My parents (all of them) have spent an incredible amount of time helping, guiding, and supporting me solely because they genuinely want me to succeed at everything. I am so very lucky for that. Thank you. And Mike, while he actually looks nothing like a cheerleader, is my biggest one. You mean the world to me.

CHAPTER 1

MY PROMISE TO YOU: TOUGH LOVE AND HOMEWORK

Welcome to your very own architectural self-help guide for your home improvement projects. You will nail down your priorities, learn how to guesstimate various budgets to compare and contrast the projects you are considering, acquire new ways of communicating to avoid biting your team's head off, and save money so you can spend more on the things you love. The end goal is to create a better living environment for you and your family that will improve your quality of life overall.

That is something we all strive for, but it is difficult to know where to begin. The tools provided in this guide will finally get you moving in the right direction and allow you to make decisions! Wouldn't it be nice to take all of the time, thinking, energy, discussions, cocktails, and Internet searches you've done thus far and turn them into forward progress? Yep, I thought so.

If you are anything like many of the homeowners I talk to each year, you are expending large quantities of your day-to-day life (sometimes for years) on any number of home project ideas in hopes that some fabulous golden nugget of information will allow you to finally make decisions on something . . . to no avail. Every new project idea, Google search, discussion with friends/family/neighbors/etc. only leads down another rabbit hole. Each convinces you that your project is more expensive than the last. You get frustrated *again*, and stop thinking about it . . . again. Rest assured: that's normal. But that doesn't make it any easier.

On top of that, if you have a spouse or partner who will also be making decisions, they, too, are flying blind through this process and most likely coming up with different ideas on which you may or may not agree.

This guide will *simplify* the process, so you can focus on the most helpful parts that you can successfully do before you hire an architect. This is your to-do list, specifically aimed at teaching you how to determine what information you need to make decisions, finalizing those decisions without hanging your partner from the roof by his or her toenails, and transferring that information to an architect in a way that will save you a lot of time and money.

It doesn't matter if you are contemplating a small remodel or building a large new home from scratch. This guide will teach you to analyze parts of your own project (big or small) so that you can understand the pros and cons of the specific goals you are trying to achieve. This information is not specific to a single type of project or locale. That way, you don't have to extrapolate the information to make it relevant to your situation. You will be able to analyze what you are trying to achieve, then parcel out and modify specific parts and pieces until it feels right for you. Then you repeat the process as necessary until you hone in on your goals based solely on your needs and budget, using pricing information you learn to define yourself and that is specific to where you live. How is this possible? Because I will teach you how to determine your own variables that you will then use in your own equations so they are tailored to you.

Once you have the tools to actually make some decisions, you can FINALLY evolve in a positive direction. In hopes of categorically convincing you of the remarkable effects properly utilizing this guide will have on your project, I will demonstrate what your process will look like both with and without the information provided:

The typical abridged process without using the information in this guide:

✏ You and your partner go in circles about various options and get stuck on the same points over and over again.

✏ You interview and select an architect. You explain your ideas but have no idea what any of it might cost or what has to happen to make all or some of your goals a reality.

✏ Your architect asks for some indication of your budget, but your response is that you won't be able to make decisions on priorities until you have some notion of what things cost.

✏ Your architect warns that this typically leads to multiple rounds of design drawings ($$$). She reiterates that it is uncommon for someone to end up proceeding with their entire wish list and stresses the significance of providing a list of priorities in order of importance and an approximate budget threshold. This will allow her to include as many of your priority items within the budget constraints as possible . . . as opposed to drawing your entire wish list just to see what it costs.

- You reassure her that you know a guy, who knows a guy, who said you would probably be able to get everything you want.

- You're the boss . . . So your architect draws up some options that include your entire wish list. You pick one you absolutely adore and happily skip off to show your friends and family what a wonderful new home you will soon have.

- You give the drawings to a few contractors for pricing.

- You receive the pricing and are shocked and disheartened to learn how much it costs.

- Your brain begins to add the architectural fees, engineering fees, permit fees, etc., to the pricing information you just received, and you realize you can't afford the shiny, sparkly design you fell in love with.

- You sadly cut back on various items, pay your architect to redesign everything, and go through the same pricing exercise again (and possibly a third time because you want to add back in just one or two deleted items you can't live without).

- You begrudgingly increase your budget to get those "must haves," which pushes the boundaries of your comfort level. It dawns on you that the money you just spent on the second round of design options could have gone a long way toward getting a few of those desired items, but instead you write another check to your architect.

- You ultimately have a design you can afford, but since you were not able to provide any budget-versus-priority information to your architect until now, you started with shiny and sparkly but now have a matte finish along with a lot less money to spend on your project.

✏ And that is just the BEGINNING of the lengthy process that is your remodel . . .

This is the typical abridged process using the information in this guide:

✏ You and your partner each brilliantly break out in order of importance what you believe to be the key elements of your project.

✏ You then come together to discuss your awesome ideas and agree on a few different options you are interested in learning more about.

✏ You use the spectacular advice in this fabulous guide to determine that Option 1 costs approximately $X, Option 2 costs about $Y, and Option 3 costs around $Z.

✏ You agree that Option 1 is way too expensive, but you wonder if you can get part of Option 1 with Option 2 for $N amount of money.

✏ You hire an architect.

✏ You tell your architect that your preference is Option 1, but you used an incredible book to learn how to crunch some basic numbers, and if it actually does costs $X then you aren't comfortable with that. You explain which parts of Option 1 are most important, that you like Option 2, and that Option 3 is your backup if you can't afford 1 or 2. This small golden nugget of information provides the priorities and budget assumptions needed for your architect to skip ahead past multiple rounds of costly design iterations. The biggest difference between this example and the previous one is that you were able to get to the same exact point WITHOUT paying for numerous rounds of drawings and wasting months of valuable time.

- ✏ Your architect provides a few designs combining Options 1, 2, and 3 so you can evaluate each and their associated guestimates.

- ✏ You and your partner are able to make forward progress, finalize decisions, and go to your favorite restaurant to celebrate your ability to work as a team!

See the difference? There is a right way and a wrong way to go about this process. Let me rephrase that: there is an expensive way and a less expensive way to go about this process. No, I retract. There is a right way and a wrong way to go about this process. Please opt to get your ducks in a row before you start. It will make a massive difference to everyone involved (as you will soon see), especially you.

I am a licensed architect with over eighteen years of experience in demystifying this process for clients. I've also done work on my own house, so I, too, know what it is like to be in the check writing position. Additionally, I've done enough actual construction to know that I prefer not being the one wielding the hammer, though I have the utmost respect for those who do. I run my own architectural design firm, which means that I deal with every single facet of the entire lengthy process.

Over time I have seen the many different ways people go about this process and deal with the stresses and uncertainties that accompany it. I have seen hundreds of different scenarios unfold and have carefully studied how the homeowners, contractors, engineers, city officials, and other architects deal with challenges in their own way and from their own perspective. I want to share that knowledge with you to help you avoid avoidable difficulties.

The advice offered here is not what you would normally find in a book about building or remodeling a home. It deals both with practical details and emotional challenges that happen over and over in every project. X leads to Y, which tends to cause emotion Z. Every architect has seen it a million times. I'm cluing you in on how to properly prepare for X and Y, offering suggestions on how to deal with emotion Z, and sharing how others have successfully accomplished both as well.

This guide isn't intended to replace your architect. Knowing how incredibly multifaceted the process is, there are some things I believe homeowners can and should do on their own to better prepare, while some things are best left to the professionals. I have thoughtfully picked apart the various elements that help make a project successful and identified those that homeowners could solve on their own if given the right tools. This guide is indeed that necessary tool belt.

(This leads me to a side note. From now on I will refer to architects as female in lieu of the tedious "he or she" and "him or her," not because I think women make better architects . . . well . . . I digress.)

This guide is specifically intended for those of you who have just started the process and have yet to engage an architect or contractor. It will get you from your kitchen chair to signing a contract with an architect. The reason this ends where your architect begins is because every architect does things a little differently and will guide you with her capable hands in the way she has found best suits her clients. With her you will have guidance. You do not have guidance now. Or, at least, you didn't before you picked up this book.

I will walk you through the overall process and strongly recommend (require) that you clean the crap out of your house before you start. I'll also show you how to determine what your needs are and teach you how to crunch numbers in a way that lets you assign value to those needs, allowing you to make decisions. You will learn how to build your team of professionals and how to expound in painful detail on all that you've learned to your architect to save everyone heartache and save you money in the end. How do we do this? Homework. This is my promise to you.

So what I need you to do is trust me. I won't let you down. Walk through this process with me (even if you think parts of it are nuts), present this information to your architect, and I guarantee you will be light years ahead of where you are now. I want to get you excited about your project! I want you headed into this amazing experience inspired, full of ideas, and confident in your ability to dictate the outcome! So, if you were wondering where to start, you just did!

CHAPTER 2

BEGIN BY COLLECTING INSPIRATION FOR YOUR PROJECT

I *want to inspire you to tell a story* and to create an environment where that story can be told, shared, and enjoyed by others. The most successful way of turning your home into a wonderfully unique personal haven is by creating it such that it tells *your* story. Why do you think everyone loves images of amazing lofts created inside timeworn factories or old barns converted into beautiful farmhouses? It isn't because we enjoy spending four trillion extra dollars trying to waterproof them and keep cold drafts out. It is because spaces like those evoke feelings. They tell a unique story. It doesn't have to be an old barn to evoke feelings. It does, however, need to tell a story. That story is your story.

As an architect, I'm in the "people pleasing" business. If you are happy, then I am successful. You will be happier if you can take time to determine what will make you happy, and then help me understand those elements (Architecture Self-Help 101). Think about it . . . people default to copying Pottery Barn catalogues because they see something that inspires them. Ikea has taken this one step further by creating three-dimensional versions of these catalogue pictures in their showrooms where the average person can see, feel, touch, and ultimately buy the checklist of things that evoked that initial inspired feeling. However, when you get it (whatever IT is) home, the shiny, sparkly feeling tends to fade, either when it quickly begins to wear (you get what you pay for) or when you see the exact same checklist in your neighbor's house and suddenly the magic goes POOF! The magic goes poof because your home isn't telling your story. It is telling the story of a few people who sat in a conference room somewhere and decided that the "IN" color this season would be fuchsia and that post-post-midcentury modern-ish would make a comeback . . . and because, most importantly, these were the things that would ultimately make the most profit.

Don't get me wrong. There is nothing wrong with feeding your Pinterest habit. Hey, I do it, too. We all need a little architectural foreplay to get us in the mood to remodel. Just take the time to see past the home catalogues that make their way into your mailbox, look a little deeper and longer at things, and notice what you like and don't like. You may end up discerning things you really aren't all that psyched about in the eye candy image you drooled over at first. You may realize it isn't for you after all. I recommend doing that BEFORE you spend millions on a home rather than after (just a thought).

That inspiration and energy you feel when you see something SUPER AMAZING is the energy I'm trying to get at. Grab hold and harness it! But you get exponentially better, long-lasting results if you spend the time really picking through the details, paying attention to the specifics, and allowing yourself to think outside the Ikea—I mean box. Take note of the strange little things that give you loads of joy since those things create YOUR story.

HOW DO YOU KNOW WHAT TO USE AS YOUR INSPIRATION?

Where does inspiration come from? How do you know which of the things you like will make for good archi-candy? If you have an affinity for baseball and baby back ribs, does that mean you should build a home around those things? Does that mean your house should be a big round ball smothered in sauce? We don't need to be super literal about our likes and dislikes, but it is worth brainstorming with someone who is trained to use those types of inspirations, who can help you look at them in a different light, and turn them into something you can enjoy for years to come. Here are a few examples to wet your whistle:

Example 1: How You Use Another Space as Inspiration

When I was a young girl, I was walking around my neighborhood and noticed a house to which I hadn't paid much attention on previous walks. The ground was flat on the right side of the house and then took a sharp dip down on the left. The left side of the house took advantage of this dip, and from it came a double height living room with large windows allowing one to see just how voluminous the space was. I became fascinated with that double height living room, so, I did what any small child would do: I went and knocked on the door. I thank my lucky stars that a kind older woman answered, and I asked her if I could come in and look around her home (I know, I was a strange kid). Once the door was wide open, she moved out of the way and extended her arm out as though to approve my self-invitation into her home, and I saw it. I believe this was what set me on my path to becoming an architect. When you pass through the entry foyer, you are literally standing on a bridge overlooking the double height living room below. This wasn't a modern house. In my mind, it was like a huge, dark-wood law library on steroids. I was absolutely blown away.

I am not sure how long I stood there with my mouth agape, but she eventually shuffled me further along and began her tour. It was so kind of her to take time out of her day to show me around my future profession, but when you are a kid, you don't really grasp such things. As a result, I immediately ran home to retrieve my

Example 1

11

little brother, and knocked on the door once again, so she could repeat her tour of her amazing home. I love modern architecture. I have seen some amazingly inspiring and unique homes that would cause you to use phrases like "clean lines" and "open flow." Still, if I were to build my very own home haven, and I could design anything my heart desired, I would lean toward an aesthetic resembling my old wood law library on steroids with a modern twist. That is what inspires me and why. What inspires you?

Example 2: How You Use an Object as Inspiration

The previous example was of a space that inspired me, but it doesn't have to be a physical space that brings you joy. It can be a THING as well. If we loop back to our baseball and barbeque example, I can explain how those things could be used as inspiration. Perhaps we would create an accent wall in your den completely lacquered with the many newspaper clippings you've saved over the years boasting of your favorite players' triumphs. On it could be a few shallow shelves with upturned edges to prevent your baseball collection from rolling off. Or perhaps we put a glass door on a single cabinet in your kitchen displaying your extensive barbeque sauce collection. Or maybe we create an entire outdoor kitchen and living space complete with a sixty-inch gas range, smoker, and fire pit so you can get your BBQ on. The point is, you don't have to know what you would do with your favorite objects and ideas. You do, however, have to be willing to share them with your architect if you want a unique space that tells a unique story. Those are the bits and pieces that can be used to create your home haven that can't possibly be repeated, anywhere, because they are unique—because they came from you.

Example 3: Using an Object Just Because It Brings You Joy . . . Even If It Is Strange!

You don't necessarily have to use objects you enjoy as inspiration for a design of some sort. Sometimes good old-fashioned

Example 3

displays of our most prized possessions are equally as satisfying and sometimes less expensive. A good example of an object that brings me joy is one of my favorite things in my home. It is a two-foot tall, hand-carved, wooden Thai hand puppet. She is a wrinkly, wide-eyed woman dressed in green linen with saggy boobs. The best part is that the boobs actually have strings on them, too, so you can swing them to and fro as you would her arm or leg. I have seen a million different reactions to this thing. The man who installed my new oven took one look at it and sped up his service call ten-fold to get the heck out of my apparently crazy house. My neighbors, who happen to have two-hundred different rooster sculptures scattered around their home, simply adore it. Half of my friends love it, some just laugh, and the rest think, "Eh." What really matters is that year after year, literally every time I look at it, I smile. Take THAT, Ikea! It doesn't matter if anyone else likes it. This emotion, if sprinkled throughout your home, is what will really create your personal home haven. Each piece tells a story and is like a little surprise. Everyone likes surprises. It brings life to your home. Make sure to share these inspirations with your architect to ensure they find a place in your new home.

HOW AN ARCHITECT MIGHT UTILIZE THE INFORMATION YOU GIVE HER

This next story perfectly describes how one of my clients brought me an idea (a strange one at that . . . but strange is good!) and I ran with it. He didn't know what I would do, but he had the guts to share his idea and trusted me with it.

His condo overlooks one of Seattle's historic nuggets. Highway 99 (The Viaduct) runs along the edge of the beautiful Puget Sound overlooking the Olympic mountain range. Part of The Viaduct was demolished to make way for a new transportation system in the city, and the rest will soon follow (a political topic from which I will spare you, as it has been known to actually triple the decibel level of conversations). This client once saw an image where an artist made it appear as though Godzilla was bashing through The Viaduct (which was under construction, so it appeared damaged, anyway). He thought this was the best thing since sliced bread and went on and on about wanting to find or recreate this for his home. Inspired by his strange interest in this thing that I, myself, would never have gravitated toward, I worked with a local concrete fabricator to obtain a chunk of the actual demolished Viaduct. We were already in the middle of remodeling his bathroom, so we decided to turn it into a powder room sink where the top was cut flat and polished, and the edges were left natural and rough to evoke the destruction done by Godzilla. You can see and touch the massive chunks of stone aggregate that once held up our highway. Steel legs were also designed to suggest the steel in the concrete. This type of STORY is what will create your personal home haven. He loves his sink so much that the first thing he does with new visitors is shuffle them single file into the powder room to tell the story. His story.

Don't hide these wonderful details behind copied magazine images. When you are in the process of telling your architect exactly how you want your kitchen to function, don't forget to share with her the things that grab hold of your heart strings. Those details are what make homes engaging and awesome. Don't be afraid to take your barbecue sauce collection, or whatever it is that brings you joy, to your architect as inspiration. I've had many people tell me that they don't have an opinion and want me to provide options without input. You may not have an opinion now, but talk to your architect. Tell her about yourself. Bring a few ideas to the table to kick around, and you will be surprised at how you jump in and fall in love with the story of your new home. And don't worry, we won't take it too literally. If you show up with a polka-dotted bowling shirt, you won't end up with a home that looks like the 101 Dalmatians live there.

WHY EXPLAINING THE INSPIRATIONS BEHIND YOUR PRIORITIES CAN SAVE YOU MONEY

Let's say you tell your architect to include a lot of new lighting as part of your basement renovation, so it doesn't feel like a cave. In addition, you could also describe a coffee shop you once experienced tucked away in the back corner of a public market that appeared bright and airy, even with the lack of natural light. You found yourself trying to figure out where the light was coming from, because you didn't see big light fixtures or recessed can lights all over the ceiling. It was like the space was just light and bright all on its own. Finally, you figured out that there were various types of hidden light sources pointed at walls and ceilings that were indirectly lighting the space, and it was AMAZING. Tell THAT to your architect, and you've just directed her in a straight line to a successful lighting plan for your basement. Leave that information out, and you could go through three rounds of lighting plans to get what you want. See what I mean?

You don't have to know WHAT to do with the information. Just write it down and include those memorable experiences when explaining your inspirations and goals to your architect. I realize some things might not be as tangible as, say, a toilet, but they are equally as important. You may not be able to foresee how these lists could be helpful or how to use some of these ideas. Please know that it isn't your job to figure that out. It is your architect's job. But giving her a starting point and inspirations that are unique to you can only help.

I am guessing by now you are starting to get my drift. You might be pondering which thing might be YOUR thing. You might also try to rationalize that while the previous examples are all well and good, you have no idea which of your favorite things could be used to help create your home haven. Here are a few queries to get you started. This is merely for brainstorming so you can come up with a list you can share with your architect. You must understand that just because you are putting the lists together doesn't mean they will literally find their way into your home. Trust your architect if she tells you something just won't work. There will be give and take because that is part of what makes for a successful creative process.

QUESTIONS TO HELP YOU DETERMINE YOUR INSPIRATIONS

Ready to determine what might be YOUR INSPIRATIONS? Here are a few questions to ponder, and don't worry—you won't be graded on this:

✏ Can you think of a place you've been that you absolutely loved, that left you with a feeling of peace or inspiration that you enjoy reminiscing about? Everyone has looked at photographs of beautiful places online or in magazines, but I want you to think back to a space that you actually occupied, that really had an impact on you. It could have been inside, outside, a library, a restaurant, an old train station, etc. If you had to pinpoint two or three things about that memorable space that had the most impact on you, what would they be? Make a list. Was it the lighting, the flooring, the way the windows aligned on the exterior? Maybe you loved a few unique details, or maybe a garden statue? Maybe it was a large space broken up perfectly into smaller alcoves where you could have intimate conversations. Take a minute and put yourself back in that space; look around with your mind's eye and see what you notice. Take some detailed notes about what you saw, felt, heard, smelled, or touched that impacted you the most.

✏ Now create a new list. Have you ever been in somebody's house that you loved? The previous list may have included a residence but often times it doesn't. Did you love the open floor plan or maybe the way the entry created a warm, welcoming first impression? Was it just that you saw something super unique that you hadn't seen before and thought was clever? Maybe they had an interesting piece of art that appeared to be made specifically for the spot where it hung. Even if the piece of art wasn't something you liked or would have purchased, perhaps you still thought its relationship with the building was interesting and uncommon. Create some notes about anything that stood out in your mind.

✏ If you had to think about all your possessions, regardless of whether or not they are on display or in a box, which of them evokes the most positive emotion from you? I'm not asking which of them would most likely be found at Pottery Barn or has the most monetary value. I'm asking about objects that are important to you and make you smile, regardless of whether you would ever put them out for others to experience. Maybe it's an old set of finger puppets you had when you were a kid. Maybe it's a small, interesting glass sculpture of a man's head you found at a garage sale last week. Again, make detailed notes about the specifics you like.

✏ Do you already have something you might want to incorporate but don't know how? Forget about the HOW, and just write down the inspiring thing you are thinking about. You don't necessarily have to use it, but you do at least have to write it down.

✏ Have you ever seen something that blew you away for one reason or another? Even if it has nothing to do with your home, what specifically did you like about it and why? If it was an image of a private jet, did you like it because it was ergonomic and sleek? Or did you like it because of what it stands for (financial security, tech savvy, etc.)? Whatever it is, make a note. Maybe you should have an awesome focal point in your home that stands for the same kind of sleek *idea* rather than physical characteristics . . . even if it has nothing to do with private jets.

✏ Do you have some ideas you like but that don't fit together? For example, are you dead set on building a contemporary home but love old wrap-around porches and have no idea how these two things could possibly be designed into a single home? Write it down.

✏ You can use old photos or images, written descriptions, physical objects, or anything that helps you depict an idea to your architect. Don't be shy!

You know how reading a book has this strange way of engaging your brain in a different way than a movie? The movie hands your brain the entirety of the picture on a silver platter, which gives you a temporary feeling. Once it is over, the feeling is gone, because you weren't engaged in creating anything using your own imagination. This is why we binge-watch on Netflix, right? We like the fleeting feeling we get when watching the show, and when it is over we need another fix! Books, on the other hand, grab you in a different way. You create part of the story in your head due to the lack of images. As a result, you can inherently relate to it more because you created the visual story in your head . . . so it is part YOUR story. Someone else reading the same book might have a completely different image in her head of the same characters or settings that they then relate to in their own way.

You want your home to be like the book you engage with using your imagination, only now you engage with the architecture to evoke unique feelings you can't get somewhere else. You can't get it somewhere else because it is your story, not your neighbor's. Share the ideas you've discovered with your architect. Collaborate, brainstorm, and see what wonderful, unique things she comes up with for your unique home.

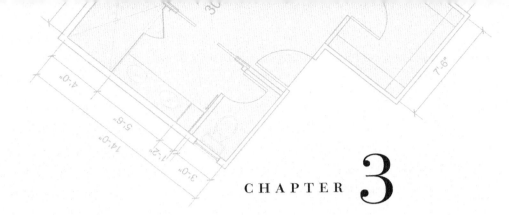

CHAPTER 3

CLEAN OUT YOUR CRAP BEFORE YOU BOTHER MODIFYING YOUR HOME

H*ow do you know how much* of a given type of space you need if you have rooms and rooms full of crap you don't even like?

Before I remodeled my home, I went through every single item and got rid of enough useless stuff to make the VIP list at my local Goodwill. You should, too. I had to do it again before my partner moved in with me in order to fit the items most important to both of us into my tiny home. More pointedly, I had to take the stuff I had already painstakingly cut in half and cut it in half again. So I have no sympathy for anyone who tells me they have spent hundreds of thousands of dollars on an addition when half of their home is currently filled with things they may very well have not set eyes on in years, and without which they may not have even needed an addition.

I'm not talking about the "if you haven't worn it in a year, throw it out" scheme. That's easy. If you haven't even done that yet, put this book away and don't come back until it's done. I'm talking about if you had five minutes to get your most prized possessions out of your house before it burned down, what would those be?

Set those aside and scrutinize everything else. Look around your home and tell me what you see. REALLY LOOK. You probably have hundreds of things hiding in plain sight that hold no real value to you. When I say, "real value," I mean things that you look at and they give you joy. These don't have to be expensive things. By all means, if you actually like that garage sale item better than the $200 gift from your friend, then bite the bullet and put your friend's gift in the TOSS pile. You could opt to put it in the MAYBE pile for now, but you need to get your game face on.

You must put yourself in a mind-set to slash and burn before you can begin anew. Again, look around. Make a list of EVERYTHING you see room by room. If you are forced to write it down, then you actually have to see it. If you did the same exercise with your eyes shut, what are the important things that you actually remember without looking? Make columns for KEEP, MAYBE, and TOSS and get slashing. Literally everything on your KEEP list has to be something you absolutely love or something for which your mother would disown you if you got rid of it. However, I would actually contemplate rethinking the latter (sorry, Mom). As the world gets more and more populated, the spaces we inhabit become smaller and smaller. Filling what should be your oasis with things of little emotional value makes no sense whatsoever.

If you need some inspiration, buy *The Life-Changing Magic of Tidying Up: The Japanese Art of Decluttering and Organizing* by Marie Kondo. I read it, and while some parts of it didn't apply to my particular circumstances, it definitely inspired me to have one more go at my and my partner's (much to his dismay) things.

If you can't do this, how you do expect to make much harder decisions about building a home? Trust me. Get your game face on and go for it. You can do it and it will feel awesome! Purging useless, unwanted items with little or no emotional value is like finally ridding yourself of a disease. You feel light, inspired, and ready to take on the remodel. Getting yourself mentally prepared for what lies ahead is extremely important. You want to begin the remodel process on the right foot, feeling confident that you just made a rash of hard decisions and are ready for battle.

You will have a lot more space once all of those useless things are gone. That space might lead to totally different priorities or opportunities. Let's say you want a media room, and your plan is to add on to the back of the house to get it. If you happened to suddenly have a lot more elbow room in your basement due to the purging, could you turn it into the media room now that you have enough space for the gang to watch a movie? Maybe you hadn't even considered it because the headroom is not ideal. Now that you have the extra space, however, would it be better to raise the house to get the needed headroom instead of adding on? Maybe that would allow you to keep the beloved garden that would otherwise have been destroyed by the addition! See what I mean?

You could have an entirely different project that could either save you loads of money or provide you with a much better home in the end. You must clear out the nest in order to assess what you have and what you need. This step is hugely important, so get moving. I'll wait here for you.

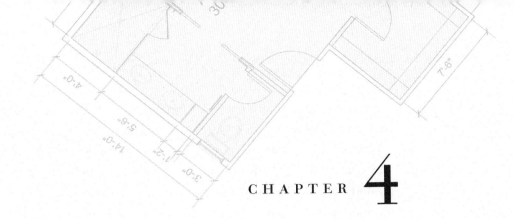

CHAPTER 4

REMODEL OR MOVE?

You are inevitably considering spending a lot of money and expending a lot of energy so I recommend that you consider all options. I'm not going to regurgitate one of those reality television shows where homeowners are given multitudes of options by well-manicured people describing ways to renovate or sell their home, all in a thirty-minute time slot. Trust me. It isn't that easy. Even if you are contemplating moving, the things you learn in this book still apply. You still need to assess your priorities and be able to do some quick number crunching to see if the house you are looking at meets your needs. If not, is it something you can afford to fix?

PUT MOVING AND REMODELING ON A LEVEL PLAYING FIELD

Going through the exercises in this book will help you put moving and remodeling on a level playing field so you have a way to compare and contrast the options and ultimately make decisions. I recommend that you go through the process and assess your options for remodeling your own home first. Then, if you are still contemplating moving, you should go look at some houses. The reason I recommend that order is because by the time you get done assessing things in your own home, you will have done the hard part. You will have a better understanding of yourself and your needs and be better at concisely summing up homes you may consider purchasing. In addition, your brain will be wrapped around the big picture, and then you'll have something to which to compare potential new homes.

It is a competitive market. If neither you nor your realtor can get you to a place where you can see how a particular home might fit your needs (maybe if certain things are changed), then off you go to the next house . . . and the next, and the next. It is a time suck for everyone involved.

Make the process more efficient for everyone by knowing what your priorities are, how much you might spend to get what you want, and how to gather enough information to know if you are in the right ballpark or not. Otherwise, by the time you visit your seventh house, the first five houses you looked at have already sold. You get frustrated at the process, and after coming to terms with the fact that you are going to have to remodel regardless of what you buy, you end up buying old number seven just because it is the least expensive (much to your realtor's dismay). Your thinking is that buying low will leave you with the most money to remodel. However, at no point did you have enough information to actually know if remodeling the cheap house will ultimately cost more than you would have spent buying and remodeling houses one through five.

Remodeling is challenging. Don't just buy into a large remodel if you don't have to. Take the time to figure it out. If you utilize the information in this guide to get a few key elements figured out, you can always pay an architect for an hour or two of her time to visit houses with you and review the list of assumptions you've come up with about the scope of work in each home. Just make sure you do your own homework first, so you can rule out a few ugly ducklings to avoid paying an architect to tell you something you can determine on your own.

HOW LONG YOU PLAN ON STAYING MAKES A HUGE DIFFERENCE

If you ARE going to take the time to remodel, I want to give you a piece of advice . . . Many people make decisions about their construction project based on resale value, so I want to bring the element of TIME into this discussion. Maybe moving has been made easier by the advent of all the newfangled technology we have now. It seems people commonly get the itch to upgrade after only a few years of living in their home. They come to me with eyes bigger than their wallets without really considering what the next five, ten, or fifteen years of their lives might be like. Our society has gotten impatient, and in my opinion, it is due to the newfangled technology (don't get me wrong, my smartphone and I are attached at the hip). However, when you are dealing with the amount of money it takes to do a remodel, let alone the amount of money it takes to do a remodel PROPERLY, you MUST take a deep breath and a good, thorough look at your future.

I really want to nail this idea home (pun intended) because:

☞ I truly believe your home should be your sanctuary.

☞ Sanctuaries are created when people take the time to really own their project and make it work for their specific needs and preferences.

☞ Specific needs and preferences fly out the window if you worry too much about resale value and disregard what will make YOU happy.

- ✏ You (rightfully so) worry about resale value if you plan on moving in five to seven years.

- ✏ If you are planning on moving that soon, do you really want to spend a large chunk of that time in the middle of a construction project?

- ✏ Last, but not least, you get what you pay for. Suppose you are contemplating settling for something subpar because you don't want to overspend. But you can't feasibly do anything that will make a massive improvement on your life with the budget that you either have or are willing to put into the property. In that case, try putting down the flashy newfangled technology and practicing the art of patience.

I bring this up because when my clients are planning a remodel for the house they plan to stay in for the next fifteen-plus years, they are making decisions for a very different set of priorities than if they were planning on moving in five years. Like investing in the stock market, this allows time to make up for the higher budget needed to ultimately get what you want. The projects are almost always better quality; things function exactly how they want them to, and they are so excited about the process because they are planning their home haven and working toward it.

While I realize it is impossible to recommend that everyone not move for fifteen to twenty years, if you are planning on moving in five, I would just make sure to ask yourself if you want to spend a lot of money to get something that may not be quite right, and if you are okay with most (if not all) of your free time being taken up by something you are not super passionate about. If you do decide to go for it, that's fine; people do it all the time. However, you could also use this time to clarify the things you really don't like about your current living situation and use that information to direct your next home search. In the meantime, you could save up a bit more money to make your next home the one in which you want to invest. You can have the home haven of your dreams; it might just take a bit of patience to really nail it.

My two cents.

CHAPTER 5

PLAN AHEAD FOR PARTNER PREDICAMENTS

I**f you and your partner are the type of people** who work well together—or even don't work well together but expect to jointly participate in the decision-making process during your construction project—then there are a few things you need to think about and be prepared for. Determining your priorities before starting your project is the single most important thing you can do before calling an architect. It will set you on a path to success and lay the groundwork from which you will be making many decisions in the months to come.

However, it is very difficult to determine your priorities if you and your partner cannot communicate properly. I want to share with you some common communication pitfalls I've seen time and time again in hopes that you can avoid them. These are stressful times; you are faced with life-altering decisions that involve a lot of money. You may not agree with your partner's desire to move three bedrooms and a kitchen in order to center the television in the living room. That's okay. Learn what you should be focusing on, how to deal with disagreements, and how to avoid many of them in the first place.

IT IS OKAY TO ADMIT THAT YOU DON'T UNDERTSTAND

I have seen many MANY couples go through this process and have taken note of how people handle different situations. Some work better than others. You need to always ask yourself, your partner, your architect, and your contractor, "Is this what you mean? No? Then can you explain it again?" You have to become a patient listener. You can't be afraid to admit when you don't understand something (construction is complicated and everyone is confused . . . you aren't alone). Let me repeat that one: you can't be afraid to admit when you don't understand something. Got it now, or shall I say it again?

AGREE TO DISAGREE

You and your partner also need to agree that it is okay if you don't agree. It is natural and frankly impossible to agree on everything, which is just fine. Let your architect help you harness the differing opinions to create a third and possibly better solution. For example, if one of you is focused on maximizing the amount of natural light in your kitchen, the other is adamant about using the available budget on a big deck and barbeque, and you are both insistent that your way is the right way, you could easily miss a solution or compromise that is staring you right in the face. For example, big glass French doors from the kitchen to the new big deck and barbeque! You get your natural light, your partner gets a deck, and everyone is happy. You are going to have to come to conclusions about your priorities one way or another. Do you want to arrive at your solutions after hours or days of hardheaded battle? Or would you rather communicate better, determine the outcomes that work for you and your family, and feel like you are all on the same team? You must become professional communicators.

WHO WILL BE MAKING THE DECISIONS?

The first order of business is to determine who is going to be making decisions during the process. Do you live alone? Do you have a partner? Will you both be making decisions? Maybe you want your kids to weigh in on things. Are you the type of person who simply must ask your sister/uncle/friend for his or her opinion on everything, every step of the way? Whatever it is, that's fine. Just have that system in place when you begin. Be aware that if you stray from that system and ask a different person to weigh in half way through the process, you will inevitably get an opinion that is not based on the thousands of decisions that came before it that got you where you are today.

I'm definitely not discouraging you from getting out there, doing your research, talking to people, seeing what others' experiences were, looking online, etc. By all means, gather as many ideas as you can until either your head explodes or you nail down your priorities. Just make sure that if you plan on asking people their opinion throughout the project that they are committed to keeping up with the entire process and being part of the conversation all along.

You don't want your architect to be 85 percent finished with the permit drawings and have a neighbor give you a million different reasons why an addition would have been cheaper than remodeling what's already there or vice versa. This neighbor won't have been privy to the 300 reasons and decisions that preceded his oh-so-thoughtful comments, and the stress you are feeling from getting construction pricing and architectural invoices could cause you to buckle. You might tell your architect to hold the boat and take a "quick look" at what the difference might be between your neighbor's brilliant idea and the thing you've been working on for the last five months. Do you know what happens then (hint: $$$)? You've just spent even more money on architectural fees and will most likely end up back where you are now. Thanks, kind neighbor.

"Neighbors" like to flex their construction knowledge muscles without taking the six days of conversations needed to get him or her up to speed on the project. Frankly, if you actually did take the time to properly bring said neighbor up to speed to make the conversation even remotely valid, merely reviewing where you've been will probably make you realize his or her suggestions are not for you.

What typically happens, however, is that the panic from the pricing and invoices I mentioned earlier paralyzes you, and you instantly turn toward what appears to be a "better" solution— your neighbor's solution. I'm sure they all mean well; however, it is highly improbable that your neighbor will swoop in, wave a magic design wand, and come up with a cheaper, faster, better, easier, get-more-for-your-money option WITHOUT having been party to the thousands of conversations you've had with your team. You must have faith that your trained architect considered many, MANY options at the beginning of the process (even if you didn't see the huge pile of discarded sketches), all of which were based on the multitude of decisions you made about your own priorities. You need to be ready for this to happen. Make a decision at the very beginning that if your neighbor wasn't in on the party from the get-go, he or she doesn't get to join in on the fun later on. Trust me on this one.

HOW WILL DECISIONS BE MADE EFFICIENTLY?

Along with determining WHO is going to be making decisions, you need ask yourself HOW decisions are going to be made during your project. Time is money during construction. Do both you and your partner need to weigh in? Are there certain things you care about and other things you don't? If so, make a list of those things. Are you willing to allow your partner to make decisions in your absence on anything else that isn't on your list? This might sound odd, but you would be surprised how often a couple begins the process with both parties fully involved, and then one of the two fades away after the first few meetings. It becomes infinitely more likely that mistakes will occur in this scenario because only half of the team is present half of the time.

Think back to that game you played when you were a kid called Telephone. Remember that one? You whisper a sentence in the ear of the person sitting next to you, they then whisper it to the person next to them, and so on. By the time that sentence reaches the end of the circle it has changed from, "Joey ate an apple for lunch," to "There's a basketball game on Saturday." Imagine if the sentences being transferred concerned a topic you knew little to nothing about. In addition, if you get it wrong, there is the stress attached to the additional money it might cost.

For example, let's say your architect explains to you that the design suggestion made by your partner (who is not present at the meeting) will cause the soffits to be so low that the casing on the adjacent windows and doors will look strange . . . and if you lower those to match, then they won't align with the siding design on your façade you've all discussed at length. Try that in a game of Telephone. Later that night you reiterate your understanding of the situation to your partner and it sounds a bit like this:

You: "So the architect explained that your design suggestion wouldn't really work because it would affect something on the siding."

Your partner: "What does my suggestion have to do with the outside of the house?"

You: "She said that the soffits wouldn't align with the casing."

33

Your partner: What is a soffit? Align with what?"

You: "I don't remember."

Your partner: "So how does my suggestion change the outside of the house then?"

You: "Crap."

Now your partner is annoyed that you can't accurately reiterate the discussion from the meeting, and you resent being put in this position in the first place. Can you tell I've seen this happen once or twice before? Then do you know what happens (hint: $$$)? You have to call your architect the next day and pay for an hour long phone conference so she can re-explain what you just went over the day before. Multiply this by fifty, and you have just lost a good chunk of your project budget.

WHAT IF ONE OF YOU HAS LESS TIME TIME TO SPEND ON THE PROJECT THAN THE OTHER?

You and your partner need to have a serious discussion about how much time each of you has to spend on the project, and if it isn't realistic for you both to be 100 percent present, then rules need to be put in place ahead of time that allow you to deal with this successfully. Don't just assume you are in it together until the end. Believe me, I'm not judging you if one of you simply doesn't have the time to be fully involved. Just get it out in the open at the beginning and plan for it. Although there are many ways of managing this situation, following are two options to consider.

OPTION 1

If you and your partner decide you will be managing the project, and he or she has little interest in anything except the end result and budget, that's fine. It actually isn't uncommon.

What IS common, however, is for the disinterested party to feel somewhat obligated to participate more than he or she has the time or inclination to and, as a result, pokes his or her head in at random times in a way that holds up the process, increases the cost of things, or worse. Even if one party readily relinquishes the throne, inevitably there will be one or two things that are "must haves," so make sure to flush those out.

Let's say you are the less interested half, and you need a home office. You have to make sure to communicate any and all "must have" details about your office to the managing partner. This is your responsibility so don't think your partner can read your mind or that something is obvious. Be redundant. Be as specific as earthly possible . . . down to the tiniest, itsy, bitsy, teensy, weensy details. If you describe your office needs as being solely a desk and chair, then don't expect anything other than that. Maybe your partner has worked with the architect to nail down the plan, elevations, and details, and the permit set is underway. If this is the first time you look at the design, you need to accept some responsibility if you are unhappy with the fact that your home office is located on the side of the house closest to the neighbor who hosts band practice every day. You must take responsibility for communicating which things are important to you, agree that the managing party has the authority to make decisions on everything else, and then live (happily) with those decisions.

You need to accept that there will be a few things you would have done differently and not harp on your partner about them. If, after every meeting he or she has with the architect, you find yourself making changes to what was decided at the meeting, this approach may not be for you. If you go this route, be ready for hefty architectural bills to revise the drawings (and don't blame your architect for it!). This is where money just flows like a waterfall out of your wallet, and no one is happy. Why? Your partner is frustrated that you keep changing things but won't make time to be part of the process or respect his or her decisions.

You are frustrated with the increased architectural fees and having to change things you think should have been obvious. Additionally, it is difficult for the architect to constantly make large changes and keep the whole project cohesive and flowing together properly. If, by chance, you are not the disinterested party but your partner is, feel free to hand this chapter over as required reading.

OPTION 2

An alternate way of dealing with an absent partner is to delegate one party as the main point person between the couple and the architect, with the understanding that both will make decisions later when their schedules allow. I have seen this work very well if this is the obvious intent from the beginning and if the person doing the communicating either is, or temporarily becomes, an obsessively diligent communicator. If you are the one handling the emails, calls, meetings, etc., you must fully and accurately reiterate all of the information to your partner. This means compiling all of the emails, meeting minutes, drawings, etc., so you and your partner can later comb through everything you covered with the architect. You then make decisions together, and that same communicator then reiterates those decisions back to the architect.

What you want to avoid is one person having one conversation or meeting with the architect, the other person following up, and having information fall through the cracks. You can see how this could cause problems. This inevitably leads to . . . wait for it . . . (hint:$$$!) yep, you guessed it: more changes and more fees. If you have a type-A personality and you enjoy being organized, delving into the details, and asking WHY so you can answer all of the questions coming from your partner who wasn't at the meeting, then this job is for you. I wouldn't do it personally (that just isn't my personality) but I have had clients who have pulled this off with flying colors.

Don't get me wrong. I do believe the best approach is having all parties involved in all of the details all of the time. I just realize that in today's crazy world that isn't always possible. Just be honest with yourselves about this ahead of time and make sure your priorities are clear. Then determine how you will provide, in an efficient and crystal clear manner ahead of time, the information your team will need.

DEVELOP WAYS TO GET PAST THE GRIDLOCK

The next hot item is finding a way forward when you and your partner reach an impasse. It is okay to disagree and frankly inevitable. It is also not the end of the world. Making hundreds of decisions that affect future decisions that cost a lot of money is stressful.

Once during a client meeting, the couple I was working with couldn't agree on something. They both had valid points, and it was clearly something they were going to need to discuss at length. One said to the other, "This is obviously something we don't see eye to eye on, and it is important that we be aligned on this. Let's discuss it tonight and get back to Stephanie with our decision." They understood ahead of time that it is okay if they don't agree and had a plan in place for that. I later asked them how they finally made their decision, and they told me they actually use "bargaining chips" for these types of challenges. They each had five chips (poker chips), and they could opt to use one of them to override the other to resolve something they disagreed on. "You can't have too many or it won't work, because you could keep one-upping each other and get nowhere," they explained.

If you really want the range oven in the island and your partner wants it against the wall, you can use a chip to resolve the dilemma. Just be sure you're okay with the fact that you might have to accept the four-burner range instead of the six-burner one you wanted if your partner uses a chip to knock your preference off the table. This is just one way that one couple resolved their disagreements. You may have another way that works for you, but agree in advance on how to resolve these types of impasses.

BE PATIENT AND LEARN HOW TO LISTEN

The ability to communicate well during this process is key. Be patient and practice the art of listening. It is so important that all parties involved feel they have been heard. Your project won't last forever, so make a conscious decision to control how you communicate during this process even if it is painfully difficult for you. You can always go back to being a confusing mute later. For now, know that even though this is a challenging process, the reward for doing it well is so worth the effort. A well-crafted home will massively increase your quality of life, and the better you are at communicating, the more successful you will be.

CHAPTER 6

HOW TO DETERMINE
YOUR PRIORITIES

Now *that you are communication experts*, you are ready
to begin determining your priorities. I highly recommend
that you dream big at the beginning. It wouldn't be uncommon
for one of you to love discussing all of the amazing images you've
seen and how lovely it would be to have a wonderful (fill in the
blank here) and a (fill in the blank here, too) that can connect to
the (here, too) that would allow you to have the home spa you've
always wanted. The other one might not. This might just annoy
party number two because in his or her mind all you needed was
an extra closet. Make sure you go down as many paths as you
need to at the beginning to ensure you will have the confidence
to resist the urge to make changes midproject, and so you feel
you've both been heard by the other.

If you need to compare adding a second story to adding on at
ground level, great. If you need to compare renovating the basement to adding an apartment above the garage, go for it! It is
good to get the changes out of the way at the beginning. After
all, nothing helps us decide what we like more than seeing what
we don't like. Besides, changes at the beginning cost a fraction
of what they cost later on.

CREATE YOUR LISTS

1. To get the conversation started, each person should list the things you, your partner, your kids, or Aunt Tilley (if she is to have a say) would like to include in your home building project.

    This is my favorite part! At this point I encourage you to get it all out. Write everything down regardless of whether you think it should be part of the immediate project or is within your budget. You might surprise yourself or your partner with what you deem important or unimportant. Even if your focus is on a kitchen remodel, your husband might want a deck, which wasn't part of the original project. That deck might fit nicely with the French doors you are in love with but didn't consider feasible because you have no deck.

    Include it because if you both realize that something you hadn't discussed before could bring great joy, it is worth exploring. Even if you decide it isn't enough of a priority to be part of this project budget, your efforts aren't wasted. When you eventually share your priorities with your architect, the French doors and deck could be listed as "nice to have but we don't have the money for it right now." She might suggest hiding a framed door opening under the sheetrock (and avoid locating electrical and plumbing in that location) for future French doors that will lead out to a future deck in phase two. We will cover phasing a construction project later, but include EVERYTHING to begin with, and we can weed things out later.

2. Put the items on the list in order of importance. This part is extremely important. This sets the framework for months and months of decision making later. The sheer quantity of decisions you will have to make is truly astounding, so why not make it easier on yourself by predetermining your order of importance early on?

After you both laugh off the French-doors-out-to-the-big-deck idea that you know you can't fit in your project budget, go back and include it in your list of priorities; just note it lower on the list. Or, as I mentioned before, you can include it in the "nice to have but we don't have the money for it right now" list. You can (and should) create your own lists and categories that make sense for you and your circumstances. You might have a "if Frank's mom moves in with us" list. You might have a "once Samantha goes away to college" list. Think about what your future needs will be and create your lists based on that.

The only way your architect can make educated suggestions or recommendations is if she knows all your priorities to begin with. The benefit to making it clear to her that an eating bar is higher on the list than, say, a big soaking tub is so she knows where to focus her efforts. She doesn't need to spend her time (or your money) designing that dream deck, but she can easily design the kitchen such that there is space planned for the future French doors.

3. Now it gets interesting . . . Everyone comes together and shares their lists with one another with the end goal of creating one list. If necessary, you can create an alternate list of things you don't agree on and move on. Don't get stuck on any one thing too soon, because once you begin crunching numbers (which we will discuss in a later chapter), you will inevitably revisit this list and possibly change it.

   Trust me: it isn't worth fighting to the death over your double oven just yet. That would be like heatedly arguing that your preferred vacation destination, Paris, would be better than Tokyo, your partner's preference, only to later receive an invitation to your family reunion taking place at the same time as your vacation. It's worth discussing Paris and Tokyo, but just know that there are factors soon to come that you aren't even aware of yet that could affect the circumstances.

So take everything in stride. Keep in mind that you might have to do this in more than one sitting or maybe get a babysitter for the day and go hang out at your local coffee shop. Whatever you do, be aware that this takes time, so you must create the space in your life to do it properly!

NO JUDGING!

I encourage you to hear each other out and decide ahead of time that this isn't a time to argue. Again, create a list of things you don't agree on, if necessary. If you hate the fact that your wife keeps her bike in the front living room, don't assume that creating a mud room off the back of the house with a cool new bike rack will resolve that issue. Ask her WHY she likes keeping it in the living room and not the garage. You might be surprised to learn that it is because it saves her a few minutes on her way to work each morning. (And with two kids, every second counts.) Knowing this, you both may collectively decide to get up ten minutes earlier instead of building a mud room.

See what I mean? Don't just add a mud room because you assume it will solve an issue without discussing the issue. Always ask WHY, and first see if there are agreeable non-construction solutions to some of the issues you are trying to solve. This will help you nail down the actual challenges on which the construction project needs to focus. Weeding out these issues that you can resolve in other ways will save you thousands of dollars, so make an effort to really LISTEN to one another and talk things through. Getting to the reasons behind the wish-list items will make a huge difference in the long run.

DON'T FORGET TO THINK LONG TERM ABOUT THE LONG TERM

Following are a few questions to get you thinking ahead.

✏ How long do you anticipate living in this house?

✏ Are you going to retire here?

✏ Do you or anyone who might live in your house need special physical assistance? If so, do you currently have stairs that if climbing them proved difficult, half the house would not be readily accessible?

✏ Do you have an entrance to your home on the front, back, or side of the house without steps?

✏ Is it worth designing your kitchen or bathrooms such that they could be easily retrofitted to accommodate a wheel-chair later?

✏ Should hallways be designed slightly wider than you might first anticipate, also in consideration for future wheelchairs or walkers?

✏ How might you use your child's bedroom once he or she has flown the coop? Would using that space differently alleviate the need for certain additions, and is it worth waiting for?

✏ Do you need to add a separate wing onto your house, or at least a bedroom/bathroom, that can be acoustically separated for when your kids visit with new grandbabies? Would you ever rent that area out when the grandkids are older and the separate wing isn't necessary anymore?

✏ Do you plan on having kids (or more kids) such that you should plan for extra bedrooms? How comfortable are you having those bedrooms on a different level of the house from your bedroom?

✏ In a few years will you be required to take over hosting the big family holiday party?

☞ When you retire, are you interested in writing a book or learning how to play the piano? How much and what type of space might be required to do that successfully?

☞ Have you considered things like solar panels that would eventually pay for themselves and save you money in the long run?

☞ Do you plan on doing a lot of gardening? If you would like to collect rain water for your plants, are you installing a type of roof that will leach chemicals into the water?

You MUST think as far in advance as possible so that five years after your massive, multiple-phased construction project is complete, you aren't forced to move because you didn't consider these types of needs.

DON'T ADD THINGS TO YOUR PROJECT FOR THE WRONG REASON

I would be remiss if I didn't include this piece of advice regarding determining your priorities: don't add things just because you can't figure out how to make something work. If your only goal is to remodel your kitchen, but you tell your architect you also want to move the laundry room to the basement (because in your mind that's necessary in order for you to fit everything you want in your new kitchen), do you know what your architect hears?

That you want a:

☞ laundry room remodel

☞ kitchen remodel

☞ added work in the basement to get the new laundry room to fit.

Had you just given her your list of priorities, which included fitting both a refrigerator and separate freezer in the new kitchen (laundry room was never actually a priority at all), she may have found a way to use the back half of an adjacent closet to make room for everything and leave both the laundry room and the basement as is. The money saved by not moving a laundry room could be used to buy that beautiful dresser you had your eye on, making up for the lost closet space. And there would have been enough left over for a weekend getaway during construction (or at the very minimum, to buy my book for all of your friends). Make sense?

Put your priorities together in order of importance, and don't add something just because you think it is the only way to make something else work. If something isn't a priority, keep it that way. Let your architect figure out how to cost effectively make your priorities work. Don't worry; we will make suggestions if we see something you must consider.

WHEN YOU BEGIN CRUNCHING NUMBERS, REMEMBER THIS...

The preceding initial ideas you determined will be what you use to begin crunching numbers. I will go into how to do this in Chapter 9. You will most likely have a few different projects that you want to compare and contrast. Determining some guesstimates on various options (especially the ones you don't necessarily agree on) will give you that extra nugget of information that will go a long way in honing in on what is important and what isn't.

When you first pick up your calculator, realize that it is possible (or at least common) that this first round of priorities will not be what you ultimately give your architect. Heck, even if you are super human and your initial list of priorities is exactly what you give your architect, it is possible (and again, common) that it won't be what you end up building once your architect has assessed the situation and provided some alternate suggestions. Know this ahead of time so you go into the process with the end goal being that you are able to rank what is important to you in a way that you can communicate to your architect.

If you want to compare going up versus adding on at ground level, great, start there. For something more complicated, like utilizing a bedroom to enlarge your kitchen and if you will have to add on to the house in order to do it, there are a few more pieces to the puzzle but it is still doable. Don't convince yourself that unless you have an architect provide you with a design for your specific needs that your hands are tied and you have no way of making any decisions whatsoever. I also go into this in greater detail in Chapter 9 as well (along with offering specific examples). But to describe the general process using the kitchen example: you will learn to crunch some numbers based on renovating the interior rooms only, and then crunch different numbers for adding on so you can compare the two. If you have the money to do either and remain at an impasse, you still have plenty of other obvious factors that you can consider that don't require an architect:

✏ Will losing a bedroom hurt the value of your home too much?

✏ Will either guesstimated budget price your home out of what's common for your neighborhood?

✏ How long do you anticipate living in the house? If you plan on staying fifteen-plus years, maybe the more expensive option makes more financial sense than if you were just planning on staying five-plus years.

✏ If you do add on at ground level, what has to go in order to make that work (your garden, a deck, a garage, a concrete stair to your basement) and how does that affect your decision?

✏ Is your heat source sized to handle the added area? Most likely it isn't, so you need to keep in mind there will be added cost to heat the space that won't be a factor if you are just renovating and not adding on.

This first round will give you a practice run crunching numbers on something you are not super committed to just yet. If you take my advice and decide ahead of time not to get attached to what you initially begin crunching, you can look objectively at a few different options. It is easier to learn how to play poker when you aren't playing for money, right? The same goes with these initial comparisons. You see them differently when they aren't charged with emotion. When it comes to money people sometimes feel the need to be exact. They literally get stuck and are incapable of moving on to the next step because they don't believe that what they are doing is accurate. Well, let me give you a hint: it isn't accurate. In fact, if you are looking for exact numbers, put the book down and step away from the calculator . . . this isn't for you.

This first round is also to give you a general understanding of how to put things on a level playing field (compare options apples to apples) so you can make decisions. If you can determine that your bedroom/bathroom addition will cost four apples and a new kitchen will cost six apples, you have a way of beginning the conversation even if the numbers aren't precisely accurate. When you begin to understand the value associated with various options, you have a means of fine tuning your list of priorities.

Nonetheless, there will be many scenarios where you won't have enough information to make definite decisions. No matter how much number crunching you do, it will be nearly impossible to account for all the factors involved. That is what the architect is for. The end goal is to take your temperature on various options based on your assumptions. You then take the various options AND the associated assumptions to your architect. This will allow your architect to get inside your brain in order to skip ahead a few steps and save you time and money. This gives your architect an understanding of what you want and how that might change if the perceived value of your priorities is incorrect. Being CORRECT isn't paramount in this process. Being able to communicate your priorities and the assumptions that lead you to those priorities will make this a successful process.

CREATE YOUR INSPIRATION IDEASPACE

Everyone has a different name for this (image board, inspiration board, idea books, etc.), but they are all essentially the same thing. An inspiration ideaspace is a physical or online diary of things you have seen that inspire you and that you may want to incorporate into your project. It could be anything from a photo of an entire house to a specific paint color.

Whatever IT is, inspiration is at the heart of it. This inspiration gives direction and serves as a form of communication. As you move through the process, you will modify the inspiration ideaspace as your priorities change, giving you a new direction. For example, let's say you collected numerous images of traditional colonial-style homes (because that is the general feel of your neighborhood, so you began the process with only that in mind). But recently you saw a few examples of midcentury modern homes that you like better. What happens now? You swap out the images. Don't throw them away because inevitably you may want to refer back to them for something. However, your inspiration ideaspace should be something you can readily change and look at every day to keep you inspired and focused on the end goal. Additionally, you shouldn't assume that your partner knows what you mean when you say you like craftsman details. Your definition of craftsman details may or may not be correct or could be totally different than what his or her definition is. Images speak a thousand words.

There are websites you can use to create your inspiration idea-spaces: Pinterest.com, Houzz.com, Instagram.com, Google+, and many more. You can also cut pages out of magazines and pin them to a cork board or paste them in a book if you aren't super excited about the Internet. It just needs to be something you can easily refer to and modify that will create the visual eye candy that helps capture some of the ideas you've been thinking about, gets you inspired, and keeps you on track. If you are so inclined, sometimes keeping images of things you don't like can be just as useful and descriptive as images you do like. If you get a strong retching sensation when you see a certain something, that's worth noting. Again, this exercise is also partially to transmit ideas to your architect; the more information she has, the better. Be as detailed as possible and have fun with this!

✏ Gather images of everything you love and would like to at least give a nod to in the next few discussions. Don't forget: *everything* is to be included in the first round. It is your wish list. No judging yourself or your partner. If you want a new second story, add images of second stories you like. If you want a chicken coop, a chef's range, a steam shower, or maybe a house made from a shipping container like the one you once saw online, include it. This initial phase is about dreaming big and getting inspired. Even if you don't end up using an actual shipping container, maybe you'll use corrugated metal somewhere as a wink toward the metal container. Or maybe you just like the idea of repurposing something, in which case you might create a large dining room table out of old reclaimed wood. However, if you don't include the image of the shipping container at all just because you would never actually build your home using one, your architect won't be given the opportunity to uncover if it is the actual metal you like, the idea of using reclaimed materials, or any other bits and pieces that might make for good archi-candy. See what I mean? Everything stays.

✏ Go through the images and make notes on what you like or don't like about each image. Physically make your notes ON the images if they are printed. If they are online, you can use a program like an image editor or Adobe Acrobat PDF editor to make your notes. Some of the websites (like Pinterest.com, Houzz.com, etc.) allow space for notes without having to use editing software. In a month you won't remember why you saved the image if you don't jot down your thoughts. You could merely circle things or make extensive notes. The more information you provide the more value you will get from it.

✏ Make the images easily visible and changeable. Revisit them daily. If you can print it out and have it up around the house, that is ideal. I've seen families use a temporary cork board where everyone (including the kids) could pin images and vote on their favorites. The more collaborative the effort the better.

✏ Don't throw anything away. As I mentioned before, keep all of the images you picked for the project, even if they don't apply anymore. You may need to refer back to an image for any number of reasons. As your ideaspace progressively changes, it is also useful to remind yourself of what you don't like anymore. It helps to reassure you that you like what you have selected and retells the story of your mental process that got you where you are. It is like a decision diary. It is very common to have a midproject panic and wonder if you made the right decision on this, that, or the other thing. You should have confidence that you came to your conclusions through careful analysis, thoughtful conversations about a variety of options, and sheer unalloyed brilliance. When that fails, go back to the things you removed from the inspiration ideaspace to help refresh your memory of your thought process. It is equally as important to have a record of WHY you made the decisions as having the actual decisions specifically for this reason.

ALWAYS CONTINUE TO UPDATE YOUR IDEASPACE

After each round of number crunching you will want to update your ideaboard so that it reflects your current set of goals. You will do this as many times as necessary until you get to a stopping point. The reason I am saying "until you get to a stopping point" and not "until you've made all of your decisions and you know exactly what you are going to do" is because a stopping point can be a few different things. A stopping point could be that you have your ducks in a row and are ready to rock and roll, but it could also mean that you've come to an impasse. More specifically, suppose you really want to add a second story but your partner really wants to add on at ground level instead. You've crunched some numbers, only to conclude both options have merit and now you are stuck—you are at a stopping point.

But this doesn't mean you've failed. Why? Because it is okay to disagree. This information is still immensely valuable and will save you money. Even if you are at an impasse, you are still able to spell out in great detail what your priorities are (even if they are for two different projects), and you've assigned value to those priorities. This will allow your architect to assess your assumptions and provide more detailed feedback that will help clarify things enough for you to pick a direction. She might tell you that your assumptions for the first options were incorrect because you didn't think about X, Y, and Z, leaving the second option as the only viable path. She could tell you that if you go with the first option but tweak it ever so slightly, you can actually get most of both options for only a bit more money. Your job isn't to come to the table with all of the solutions. Your job is to come to the table with all of your priorities in order from most to least important and have a guesstimated value associated with them so she can help you properly evaluate how to proceed.

Once you've gone through a few rounds of number crunching and made any necessary changes to your list of priorities and ideaspace, you will want to begin interviewing architects and contractors. See Chapter 11 on building your team for more information. The reason I suggest doing some homework first is because everyone involved will get more out of that initial meeting if you come prepared. This is also a valuable opportunity for you to test your assumptions and learn about possible challenges you hadn't considered. They are going to say things like, "That sounds good, but have you thought of doing it this way?" Or, "If you combined both of these, you could save some money." Or, "Your supertraditional, one-story home might look a bit odd with a large, modern black box as a second story. Are you sure that's what you are looking for?" Either way, most likely the discussion will make you think about new options and you may modify some things as a result. Ask questions like:

- ✏ $X is the price per square foot I was using to make my assumptions. Does that sound about right?

- ✏ Does what I'm describing sound realistic for the budget I've come up with?

- ✏ Do you have other ideas?

- ✏ Is it possible to have my cake and eat it, too?

About this last question, as much as no one likes to hear bad news, it is better to know now if what you are considering isn't realistic. Also, you definitely want an architect that has it in them to tell you things you don't want to hear and give it to you straight. It's hard and no one likes doing it, but necessary, nonetheless.

Don't feel discouraged if you need to scratch what you've done and start over. I've said it before and I'll say it again: it is much less expensive to change things now than later when you are midprocess. Additionally, the more you share with the architects, the better equipped they will be at assessing the true scope of the project. This will allow the architects to provide more accurate estimates for architectural fees (which gives you a better idea of the overall project cost). Moreover, both the architects and contractors can determine if this project fits with their current schedules and, frankly, if they want the job in the first place. Trust me, you aren't the only one doing the interviewing during these meetings! Everyone wants clients who are actively trying to educate themselves about the process. Projects with better-prepared clients are typically more successful. Happy clients can lead to referrals, which lead to more happy clients. These are the types of clients we want, and it only behooves you to have us fighting over you!

LET'S REVIEW THE PRIORITIES YOU WILL SHARE WITH YOUR ARCHITECT

Once you have incorporated what you learned from your interviews and made all necessary revisions to your priorities, budget, and inspiration ideaspace, you are ready to hire an architect. Before she gets started, you want to give her a copy of your priorities and budget (don't give her the only copy of anything. You should always keep a record of everything for yourself). Let's recap what those are and what they should look like:

1. Do you remember the inspirational items you determined in Chapter 2? I realize that was eons ago, but they are extremely important, nonetheless. Now that you have done all of this work honing in on your priorities, review the inspirational items you included and determine which, if any, still have a charge associated with them. If you still get excited about that old train station you saw once, then it stays. Do whatever you need to do to depict these inspirations in a way that feels true to you. The Internet provides a myriad of images that can be used as examples, but you can also describe something in writing. You just need to be as descriptive as possible.

Don't be afraid to pull out that finger puppet collection you love as well. Take photos and provide that in the package you give your architect with a description of specifically what you like or don't like about it. Don't chicken out. If something really resonates with you, at the very least have a discussion with your architect about how it might be incorporated. I guarantee she would be thrilled at the opportunity to do something creative. I know what you are thinking. Creative means expensive. If it lessens your anxiety, you can explain in excruciating detail that this information doesn't give her carte blanche to go nuts and turn your house into a finger puppet museum.

2. Provide your list of priorities in order of importance. Include whatever assumptions you've made that allowed you to finalize this information. This can include images, Excel files, graphs, or just a list with associated verbiage. Type-A personalities can really have a field day with this. Have at it! Your architect just needs to understand what you want and be given the opportunity to correct any erroneous assumptions you may have made in order to clarify the scope before she starts. This is so very valuable, so don't skimp on the information!

3. Provide a copy of your inspiration ideaspace to your architect. I have shared Pinterest Boards, Houzz ideabooks, or Dropbox folders with clients, and all have worked wonderfully. If you have a physical board with images pinned to it, you can take a photo of it or of each individual image. Sometimes this method makes your handwritten notes on the images in the photo difficult to see. When you save an electronic copy to share with your architect, just use the image title to jot down the words describing what's important in the photo. For example, you could provide an image of a bedroom and title it, "I like this fireplace." Just don't forget that somehow she has to be able to access the notes and thoughts associated with each image. Remember, always keep a copy for yourself

to access on a daily basis. You will continuously be adding and changing this throughout the process. This will also be what you look at when you are about to pull out your hair (or your partner's hair) midproject to remind you of how wonderful, unique, and absolutely amazing your new home will be! It will give you strength to carry on.

4. BUDGET! Once you are done reading through chapters 8 and 9 and have crunched your numbers, I want you to provide a written budget to your architect. I'm sure you included some budget information with your previous assumptions, but I want the Full Monty. This includes your construction cost assumptions, the 10-percent contingency, the architectural fees, and the other costs such as permit fees, engineering fees, or rent if you can't live in your home during construction, if those are applicable. These costs aren't going to magically go away if you opt not to acknowledge them. They will come knocking, and if you aren't smart about them, they will huff and puff and blow your house down.

I can't tell you how important and valuable this information is. Your priorities are your road map to your new home. They are your Golden Ticket . . . the crème de la crème . . .the foundation of all that is to come . . . pun intended. Having these nailed down will help with every aspect of your project from finances to mental health. Make determining your priorities your priority!

CHAPTER 7

YES, YOU CAN
ADD A SECOND STORY

So you want to know if you can add a second story to your home, and you are unsure if your foundation or main floor can hold it up. I am here to tell you that the answer is yes, and not in the "anything is possible for the right price" kind of way. I am telling you this because if you are wondering, I know you will get hung up on this uncertainty. I don't blame you . . . it is a big question, and I'm guessing you don't want to spend your time crunching numbers on something that you aren't sure is even possible.

As with other design questions, you won't know if adding a second story is right for you until you consult an architect. That's why in Chapter 8 we will only focus on the AREA you need to add or change to reach your goals not how the floorplan could be designed. I don't want you to get stuck on what is or is not possible, because there is no real way for you to know for sure without the help of a professional. That said, I have an inkling that if you are wondering if adding a second story is even possible, you might focus on getting that question answered instead of focusing on your priorities. So I am going to go ahead and clear up this issue. Yes, you can add a second story. There. I said it. Again. Not convinced? Read on . . . and when you are done with this chapter, please get back to following the instructions in this book.

I know what you are thinking. "She doesn't have any idea what my foundation is, so how could she possibly know if it can hold up a second story? Maybe I should ditch this crazy architect and call an engineer." Right? What I would like to do is educate you on why you will be able to add a second story, because if you understand the process, you will be able to advance to the next step in your remodel planning instead of spinning in circles around this fruitless question.

I have never come across a house on which I couldn't add a second story. And I've seen all sorts of interesting foundations. There's cast-in-place concrete, post and pier, and concrete block to name a few. I've even seen houses sitting on chunks of a log, on tires packed with earth, on a pile of rocks . . . shall I go on? While I'm not recommending all of these as viable options, let's break it down and look at what is actually required.

Many old homes have a mixture of "creative" construction techniques from a previous owner's friend of a friend, who knew a guy who helped with an addition way back when. Miraculously, we have managed to build second stories on all of them. The last thing you want is to spend thousands of dollars on drawings only to find out we have to knock the whole foundation down to make it work, right? Stop worrying. That is so not necessary. This simple explanation will make the whole process seem less scary.

The average foundation today is eight inches thick with rebar (steel rods) embedded in it. Building codes now have large safety factors built into their requirements, making things a lot bigger than is actually necessary to hold up your house. While it would be great to have the beefy eight-inch-thick walls, we can work with what you already have by simply modifying isolated pieces to be the required work horses.

Let's say you want to add a second story to your 1930s home. Part of your foundation is cast-in-place concrete (but it is only six inches thick), and one section is concrete block (but you are unsure if it has any grout or rebar in it . . . because you don't have x-ray vision). You can even add a log or two as a stand-in footing just for good measure to make this example really fun. In general, when you add a second story, you have a roof that sits on walls, which sit on lower walls, which sit on the foundation. We transfer loads from top to bottom, right? That's just basic physics. To be more specific, imagine a beam holding up the weight of a floor above it. Under each end of that beam is a post carrying roughly half of the weight on the beam (my old engineering professor would be mortified by this simplification, but nevertheless . . .). Those loads isolated in those two posts are called point loads. Architects trace those point loads from the tippy top of the roof all the way down to the foundation, and the structural engineer sizes and details them to make the math work out.

The reason we can add a second story to your log-footing home is because wherever those point loads are coming down, we modify the structure in those isolated locations to make the math work out. For example, if a point load is coming down on top of your six-inch foundation, the engineer might require that we break open the concrete footing below the wall and pour a new footing, 2'x2'x1' deep in that specific location and voila! Problem solved! If you have a point load coming down on your unreinforced concrete block, the solution might be exactly the same, or something slightly more complicated like temporarily propping up the house and replacing a section of the block with concrete. Even if you had a pile of old shoes as a footing, the same solution would apply there as well. Prop up the house, replace, done. While there are other factors your team will need to contend with (shear forces, up-lift, seismic retrofitting, etc.), trust me when I say that I could bore you to death with similar examples of how we might deal with any necessary structural modifications for your desired outcome. The answer will still be yes, you can add a second story.

If you were allowing yourself to get stuck on the uncertainty of your existing foundation, let me offer some advice. Don't worry about what is or isn't possible for right now. Start dreaming and crunching numbers and let your future architect worry about the structure. Take advantage of the fact that, for once, you get to do the fun part, and let someone else do the worrying for you. Now, let's get back to the rest of the book.

CHAPTER 8

YOUR HOMEWORK: DETERMINE HOW TO PROPERLY CALCULATE THE COST OF YOUR PROJECT

A QUICK SIDE NOTE ABOUT KITCHEN REMODELS

Before we get into the real meat, I want to give you a little heads-up on Kitchen guesstimating. Kitchens are typically the most expensive room in the house. I've seen people spend $15k on their kitchen by getting prefabricated cabinets and reusing their old appliances. I've also seen people spend $30k just on new appliances to bring the grand total for the kitchen to around $150k. As you can see, using a cost-per-square-foot analysis won't work for this. That said, the point of this book, as you may have picked up by now, isn't to determine the exact cost of your kitchen (or of anything for that matter). It is to see if you want to include a kitchen (or something similar) in the big picture of your remodel project or not. If ALL you are doing is a kitchen, then you will have to do more specific research on the actual cabinets, materials, appliances, etc., and this is not the book to help you accomplish that.

AND NOW, ON WITH OUR HOMEWORK

L *et's say you want to add* a second story in lieu of bumping out. But where will the staircase go? Will it go on the back of the house, which would block the view of the kids playing in the yard? If it is on the side of the house, will it infringe on the side-yard setbacks? Maybe you can put it in the space currently being used as the office. Would that mess with a structural wall in a scary way?

Sound familiar? This is when people typically get stymied and call in a contractor, who will inevitably tell you to call an architect. The architect will arrive, have brilliant ideas (we always do), show you a few options, you pick one, and have it priced out. Right? Wrong. Trust me; It is never that easy.

Why not just do a bit of number crunching ahead of time to take your temperature about a few price tags? You would be surprised how easy it is for people to begin a discussion if I just throw a few numbers on the table. Let's say you crunch a few numbers as described below and get $X for your budget. Right there you have a means of beginning a conversation with an architect about SOME sort of a path. This is what that conversation might look like:

You: We read this amazing book that suggested we crunch some numbers based on average areas and cost per square foot for construction in our area. It seems that $N/sf is about average in our area. Does that sound about right?

Architect: Yes, that sounds about right. Nice work!

You: The footprint of our house is 1,000 sf so if we added a second story it would cost $N x 1,000sf, which is WAY too much for us. Should we even bother?

Architect: What exactly do you hope to gain with the added space?

You: We would like to add a master suite, an extra bedroom for the baby on the way, and possibly another bedroom if we use the existing office space for the new staircase. And . . . does the second bedroom need its own bathroom? Will that even fit? Where would you put the staircase?

Architect: So what you are telling me is that you want a master suite and an additional bedroom for a budget of LESS than $N x 1,000sf, and if we can squeeze a second bathroom in for under that budget, great, but if not then you are okay with skipping it. Oh, and you need a home office regardless of where it ends up. Correct?

You: Yes. In a nutshell.

Architect: Just because your house footprint is 1,000sf doesn't mean you have to add a full second story (another 1,000sf). I'm pretty confident that I can draw a few options with and without an added second bathroom using less than 1,000sf to keep the budget under $N x 1000sf. Sound good?

Do you REALIZE what just happened??

MAIN POINT ALERT: DON'T MISS THIS: Had you just brought in an architect without crunching some numbers and said you needed X, Y, & Z, but you have NO idea what that would cost so you have no way of knowing where to start making decisions, the architect would (rightfully so) design a few great options without having a general direction, and this is what typically happens:

☞ Your architect draws up an addition (including schematic design, plans, elevations, etc.)

☞ You take the time to interview and meet with contractors to get pricing

- ✏ THEN find out you can't afford it

- ✏ You pay to have your architect do another round of and wait for more pricing to come back.

ONLY YOU CAN DETERMINE YOUR EXPECTATIONS

In order to guesstimate budgets, you will need the approximate cost per square foot of construction in your area for what you hope to accomplish. I explain how to determine this on the following page, and it is different for everyone. The cost of construction in your city is different than it is in the next city over. Similarly, the cost of construction in a more well-to-do neighborhood is different than it is in an average neighborhood one mile away. It isn't because contractors just up the price of everything in a more expensive area. Rather, the level of detail and quality of finishes expected in those homes is higher than their more common neighbors and therefore more expensive. As such, if you live in a posh location and a contractor tells you that she can build for 20 percent less than three other contractors with whom you've chatted, it is solely because she is referring to a level of detail from a 20-percent-less-expensive house in a 20-percent-less-expensive neighborhood. It isn't because she is magic and happens to know a guy who knows a guy.

Don't get me wrong: there is nothing wrong with 20 percent less. That might be exactly what you are looking for. It is your responsibility to do your homework and be realistic about your own expectations. Neither I nor any contractor can determine that for you.

Don't kid yourself and go with the lowest number you can find just to make your project seem more doable than it is. If you like really ornate trim around your windows and doors, and big fancy crown molding garnishing your walls, then find a few comps with those details and use those numbers (I go into this in greater detail below). Otherwise, the initial ballpark numbers will include "average" trim and molding details (from the 20-percent-less category), and when you casually mention that your preference is the gold platinum option, SURPRISE, the price will go up. You must start with numbers that accurately depict your goals if you want to get through this process unscathed. The cost per square foot you determine now will affect all of the work you do in the months ahead. Take the time to decide what is accurate for you, and be honest with yourself about it.

Okay, I'll step off my soap box now and explain what you need to do.

HOW TO DETERMINE YOUR TOTAL PROJECT BUDGET

1. You should begin by reading and following the steps in Chapter 6 on determining your priorities if you haven't already done so. You can't crunch numbers if you don't have some of your project options nailed down.

2. Now you will determine the cost per square foot to build in your area by averaging two numbers:
    » First number: We want to determine the average cost per square foot of comparable homes in your area. Find recent comps of homes similar in size and style to what you would like to build. Ask a realtor, look on websites like Redfin, etc. Next, you should be able to look on the county assessor's website (or call the office) to break out the cost of the land from the cost of the structure. You only want the cost of the house without the land so the number is not erroneously inflated. I realize it won't be exact (the assessor's numbers aren't spot on), but later we average this number with information from contractors to make it precise enough for our purposes.
        ○ For this example we are going to use a 1,500sf home that recently sold for $400,000.

- ○ If the sale price of a home in your area was $400,000 and the approximate price of the land shown on the assessor's website is $100,000, the cost of the other improvements (the house) is $300,000.
- ○ Divide the cost of just the structure by the area of house to get the cost per square foot of the house. ($300,000 divided by 1,500sf house = $200/sf.)

» Second number: Call a few residential contractors and ask what they believe to be the average cost per square foot for average residential construction in your area. Let's say he or she recommends using $150/sf for construction costs. Don't be surprised if it is actually higher than the numbers you determined above.

» Average the two numbers above: You want to average the numbers that represent comparable homes you like and the numbers you collected from contractors. This will ensure that you are not using outdated construction pricing information, while also skewing the cost per square foot toward a price point that is on par with the style and scale of the home you want.
($200/sf + $150/sf=$350/sf divided by 2 = $175/sf.)
There you have it! We will use $175 per square foot for the rest of the example.

3. Calculate the area you want to remodel. I will go into this in excruciating detail in Chapter 9, but stay with me here so we can get through the basics first.

4. Multiply the area from #3 by the average cost per square foot from #2 to get your guesstimated construction costs. For example, if you want to remodel 1,000sf, then multiply 1,000sf by $175 per square foot to get $175,000 in construction costs. I also go into this in greater detail later, but again, I want you to understand the general principle first so we are starting with the basics.

5. Sit speechless in total disbelief for a while.

6. Repeat the process to find your error.

7. Realize there was no error. This is your guesstimated cost of construction.

Now you need to consider that there are other soft costs associated with your project that you must include before you can determine the **total project budget.** The entire point of the book is to demystify the process and provide you with ALL of the necessary information, so let's just rip that Band-Aid off quickly, shall we?

Other soft costs include:

➥ 10-percent contingency

➥ Architectural fees

➥ Permit fees

➥ Engineering

➥ Other fees (described below)

Homework continued to determine soft costs:

8. Add the 10-percent contingency:

Construction costs in hand, the next step is to add a 10-percent contingency. I realize this might seem like I'm adding insult to injury, but you MUST plan for the unknown as inevitably there are surprises in every project. Depending on your particular project, the contingency could be greater than or less than 10 percent. Definitely ask your architect for her opinion before you get your heart set on a certain figure. If your overall project budget is $100,000 then setting aside $10,000, for example, may prove to be too much if you have a relatively new house and there aren't too many unknowns. (It can't hurt, however, considering unknowns are in fact, not known . . .)

In contrast, if your one-hundred-year-old house is on a steep slope, and you aren't quite sure about the quality of your foundation, 10 percent most likely won't be enough. Your contingency needs to be considered money already spent, not money you will try to save so that in the end you can upgrade something. If you look at your contingency with a hopeful eye (thinking maybe, just maybe, you can spend it on something fun), then it will be painful when you have to fork it over to remove all the rot you found upon opening up walls.

When your contractor comes to you with a surprise, it will be stressful enough given that you are dealing with something as personal as your home and a lot of money. You don't want the added stress of having to give up on one of your priorities (which one? Ack!) in order to pay for it. Your contingency should be earmarked for the unknown, unsexy things and leave it alone. Believe me when I say it will be spent on something . . . you just don't know what that something is yet.

Add the 10-percent contingency to the numbers in our example: You will thank me later . . . $175,000 x 10% = $17,500

9. Add the architectural fees:

Your construction costs will also help you guesstimate your architectural fees until you get some actual estimates from the candidates you interview. You will read all about these fees, and how to go about finding and hiring an architect in Chapter 11. For now, however, let's continue with our example. As you will soon learn, it is common for architectural fees to be anywhere from 8 to 20 percent of your construction costs depending on the city you live in, the size of your project, if your architect is providing full services or partial services, and the complexity of the design. If you are building a high-end project with a lot of custom details, you can expect to pay higher fees. If you have a relatively straightforward project and plan on picking all of your finishes and fixtures yourself, the fees go down. Until you have actual estimates from the architects you are considering hiring, let's use 15 percent of the construction cost as your architectural fees, which is quite common. Now add 15 percent. This is money well spent: $175,000 x 15% = $26,250. Notice I'm using the original $175,000 as my multiplier in all of the equations.

10. Add permit fees and engineering fees:

It is also common for engineering fees to be 1 to 2 percent of the construction costs depending on complexity, and you can count on similar percentages for permit fees. If you need a geotechnical engineer involved due to steep slopes, bad soils, etc., or a survey of your property, then you will need to get estimates for those and add them as well. For now, let's add a total of 4 percent to cover the "other fees" category. You can modify this as necessary later, but for now this will suffice.

Yes, again, add 4 percent. I realize this could start becoming painful but trust me: $175,000 x 4% = $7,000.

11. Determine and add other fees as necessary:

If you have to move out during construction, you need to start doing your research as soon as possible. Don't assume you will be able to live in your home during construction. Also don't assume you will find an apartment for normal market prices, because chances are you won't be there long enough for it to be a normal one- or two-year lease. Consider as well if you have to move all of your things out of the house and the cost of storing them. Definitely ask the contractors and architects you interview their opinion about this because you might not have thought of everything that needs to happen during construction (and the whole goal is NOT to be surprised, right?). For example, sometimes moving everything into the basement won't actually work because it will impede the plumber from accessing the pipes for the kitchen you are remodeling above. Let's add $5,000 just as a placeholder, but there is no way for me to accurately give you a guesstimate for this. You need to do your own research. That was my, "Don't sue me sentence." Did you like it?

Add everything you've estimated thus far:
$$\$175,000 + \$17,500 + \$26,250 + \$7,000 + \$5,000$$
$$= \$230,750.$$

12. This is your TOTAL PROJECT COST. Okay, the Band-Aid is officially off. Congratulations, you made it.

I'm not trying to scare you, but nine times out of ten the numbers will seem shockingly high. If you were not surprised at all, then you've just graduated magna cum laude. Put this information away, and go begin your project. If you were shocked, keep in mind that you will be using this same method to determine the costs of the other possible project options to compare and contrast. Meaning, if you use $175/sf to figure out what your partner wants to remodel, and $175/sf to determine your ideal set of changes, then you will still have a means of comparing the two things in a realistic manner, even if the price isn't totally accurate. This will allow you to start making REAL decisions about where things fall in your list of priorities.

If you think I'm crazy, you are correct, but not about this. I've lost count of how many times I, "The Professional Bearer of Bad News," have given people a guesstimate when we first met, which they waved off in disbelief and began their project with unrealistic expectations, only to be disappointed later in the process. What does this lead to? Wait for it . . . (Hint: $$$!) Yes, you've got it! This leads to higher architectural fees, because we have to modify the drawings multiple times to get you back to a design you can afford . . . once you finally determine what your budget is.

Even if you think this guesstimate is nuts, I'm sure you've heard the common phrase, "remodels always go over budget," so answer me one question: Why, oh why, then wouldn't you err on the side of having a conservative budget? Would you rather be wrong and come in under budget or be wrong and come in over budget? Trust me: this is a good place to start.

The main point of the entire book is to remove the element of surprise from this process. Even though my clients don't like being given the long list of numbers that make up the total project cost (it is inevitably higher than expected), they all agree it is better to know ahead of time than to not know at all. They like it because it answers many of the initial unknowns, and the fewer the unknowns the lower the stress level. Your goal is to gather as much information as possible so you can make as informed decisions as possible. Knowing ahead of time that you need to set aside a certain amount of money for the less sexy items will help you weed out the less important matters and focus on the end game.

CHAPTER 9

HOW TO GUESSTIMATE THE AREA OF YOUR PROJECT

(Homework Item #3 Continued)

The goal here is to get an *approximate idea* of how much space you will need to *add, change, or damage when combining the old with the new*. Notice I am lumping them all together such that you will use the same cost per square foot to calculate each one. You will be surprised to hear that sometimes (not always) it is actually cheaper to build new than it is to remodel. It all depends on the project.

Please wipe the look of disbelief off of your face. If you think about it, how long do you think it takes to cut sheetrock to fit crooked old walls, mud over the lumps and waves, hang new plumb cabinets on them, and marry it all together so the curves on the walls don't stand out like sore thumbs? Forever. How long does it take to rip it down completely, reframe, erect plumb walls and hang cabinets? It can (not always) take less time, and time is money.

Don't get me wrong; I'm not condoning just ripping everything down and starting new without considering alternate opportunities. In fact, I am a big proponent of adaptive reuse. I bring this up only to help explain why I am lumping together both the areas you might add or change. Unless you have detailed construction drawings, it is difficult to assign different values to building new versus remodeling. See what I mean? Well, actually, it doesn't matter for our purposes because, again, we are just trying to get you into a stratosphere where you can begin analyzing options in order to make decisions. I recommend you follow my instructions and lump together both the spaces that you are adding and the space that you are changing for now.

TWO EXAMPLES: BUMPING OUT VS. GOING UP

If you are anything like the other millions of homeowners trying to determine how to begin this process, it is common to feel paralyzed by all of the options in front of you. Let's look at two examples of common project types, so you can learn how to apply this knowledge to your own circumstances. I provide some floorplan options in this guide, but you can also search online or check out my website where I've stashed a bunch for your use: www.waschastudios.com.

Example 1: Bumping Out

Let's say you want to add a laundry room and a bedroom off the back of your house. You would love to add a bathroom as well, but you aren't sure if you can afford it, and the laundry/bedroom addition is the main priority. In order to add on to the back of the house, you might have to mess with the kitchen conveniently located where you want to build. But you are on the fence about including your kitchen in the remodel because it is not too bad as is and, although you can't figure out how to do it, you might be able to add on without touching the kitchen . . . or can you?

Didn't that all sound like a jumbled mess? Your options are probably similarly jumbled, right?

Well, don't worry. We will break it up into manageable pieces to which you can add and subtract to your heart's content until you nail down a game plan.

STEP ONE:

Determine the areas you want to add

We will start by determining the area of the rooms you want to add. You can use the length and width of similar rooms in your (or your sister's/friend's/etc.) house that you like, search online for average room sizes by name, use the examples provided in this book, or check out the myriad sample plans located on my website (www.waschastudios.com). Whatever is convenient for you will work for this first round, as you will soon see.

LAUNDRY ROOM: You could start with an average small laundry room of 6'x6'=36sf

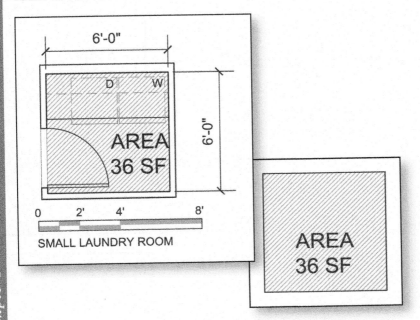

YOU ONLY NEED THE AREA FOR THIS CALCULATION. Don't worry about the layout or what goes where.

BEDROOM: An average bedroom is 12'x12'. Closets are 2' deep so let's say 2'x7' for the closet and the remaining 5' for the entry. We will use 168sf total for the bedroom. If you want it a bit bigger or smaller then go for it.

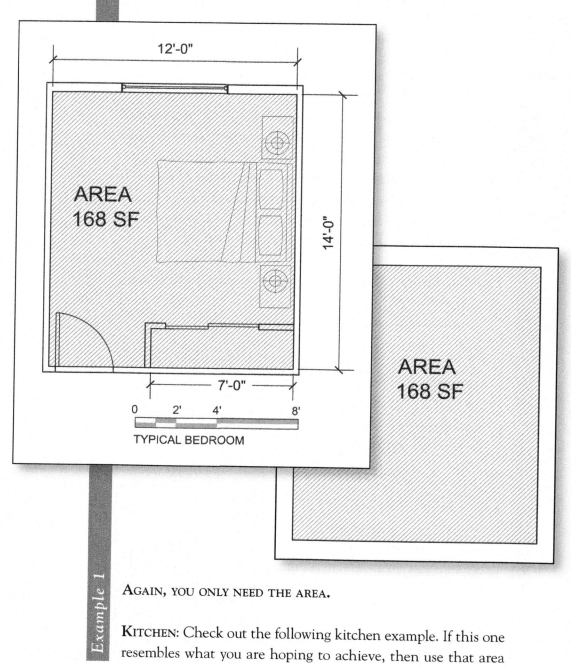

12'-0"

AREA
168 SF

14'-0"

7'-0"

0   2'   4'   8'

TYPICAL BEDROOM

AREA
168 SF

Example 1

AGAIN, YOU ONLY NEED THE AREA.

KITCHEN: Check out the following kitchen example. If this one resembles what you are hoping to achieve, then use that area for your calculations. Again, find something you like and see if you can get some measurements to use in your calculations. An average U-shaped kitchen, for example, consists of three sides containing 2'-deep cabinets. Between the cabinets there should be a minimum of a 5' space. Let's say 9'x10' works for now (90sf). If your dream kitchen is a bit bigger or smaller, feel free to use different numbers that best describe your goals. I'm not asking you which design will fit in your current home. I'm asking which design is your ideal Kitchen. Start there. Let your architect worry about how to get things to fit. Read on . . .

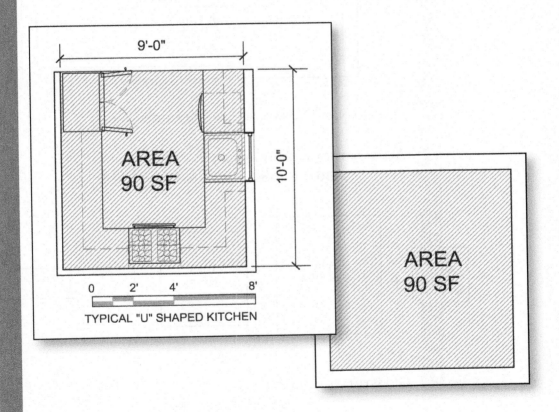

YES, AGAIN, YOU ONLY NEED THE AREA.

HALLWAY: You aren't going to get away with an addition and not have some sort of hallway, so let's say a 3'-wide by 15'-long hall for starters. If you have a 2,000sf + addition, you might need to add

Example 1

a bit more hallway. The key is to have some sort of an allowance for it in your budget.

15'-0"

AREA
45 SF

3'-0"

| 0 | 2' | 4' | 8' |

HALLWAY EXAMPLE

AREA
45 SF

YES, AGAIN, YOU ONLY NEED THE AREA HERE, TOO.

ALL TOGETHER WE ARE ADDING:

$$36sf + 168sf + 90sf + 45sf = 339sf:$$

AREA
36 SF
$+$
AREA
168 SF
$+$
AREA
90 SF
$+$
AREA
45 SF

GUESSTIMATE SUBTOTAL so far:

$$339sf \times \$175/sf = \$59,325.$$

Example 1

78

STEP 2:

*Determine the areas you are demolishing
in order to add the new spaces*

To determine the space that needs to be demolished in order to combine the old and the new, you are going to have to make some educated guesses. I realize this sounds scary, but the point is not to nail down an exact number because that is impossible at this point. Please step away from the graph paper! We need to add some money to the budget for marrying the old with the new as a place holder. If you happen to know you want to isolate the damage to a particular room (like using a bedroom to create the new laundry room and hall to the addition), great. You can use the area of that room as the "damaged space" allowance. If you know you have to demolish a closet to make way for the addition, then use the area of the closet. If you are completely unsure, I offer an alternative method below that doesn't require you to have any specific details figured out about your project in order to proceed.

I want you to think of your structure in broad terms. (See image on page 80.) Let's say the back of your house where your addition might be best located is 50' wide, and your goal is to add on such that about half of it remains untouched. For example, maybe you have two bedrooms and one bathroom on that 50' exterior wall that you don't want to damage with an addition so they maintain their windows to the yard. Look at your house and make some assumptions. Which portions should remain untouched? Which portions could change? Which portions are on the fence? Write them down and later make sure you share any of your assumptions with your architect. This number is going to be the most unknown, so don't think that by arguing until you are blue in the face you will magically be able to come up with an exact number. Don't forget, I am providing you a mathematical way (not design suggestions) of proceeding in order to compare and contrast ideas.

Example 1

79

Let's continue. You decide you want to leave the bathroom and two bedrooms on that 50' exterior wall alone but could potentially demolish the remaining half of that exterior wall to create the addition. Let's use about half of the side of the house that might be demolished (25') for our example, but you can always get out a tape measure to obtain more accurate numbers.

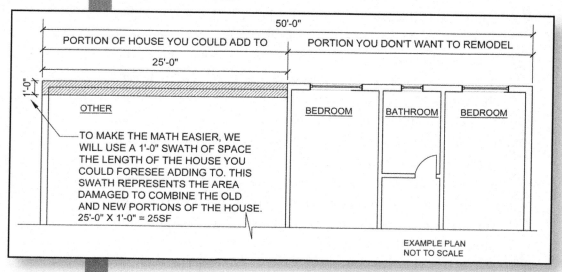

I want you to picture peeling that exterior wall off of the house for the entire 25' section. To simplify the equation, let's say we are peeling 1' of wall off of the full 25' width. If we multiply 1' x 25' we get 25sf of damaged space that will need to be fixed. Again, if you know that you want to utilize one entire room to marry the old with the new, then use the area of the room. My suggestion of peeling off a 1' section across a portion of house is a way of providing an allowance in the budget for some unknown portion of work. If you include only the addition in your calculation (without considering any damaged portions), you will be farther off than if you make an educated guess and include something as a place holder. Your job is to make those educated guesses, write them down, and include those assumptions in the information you share with your architect. For now, let's continue with the example.

Example 1

$$25'x1' = 25sf$$
$$25sf \times \$175/sf = \$4,375$$

GUESSTIMATE SUBTOTAL so far:
$$\$4,375 + \$59,325 \text{ (from earlier)} = \$63,700$$

STEP 3:
Now for the soft costs. . . .

ADD A 10% CONTINGENCY:
Now that you have a better guesstimate of your potential project costs I want you to add a 10% contingency.
$$\$63,700 \times 10\% = \$6,370$$

ADD 15% FOR ARCHITECTURAL FEES:
$$\$63,700 \times 15\% = \$9,555$$

ADD 4% FOR OTHER FEES:
$$\$63,700 \times 4\% = \$2,548$$

ADD SOME AMOUNT FOR RENT AND STORAGE:
$$\$5,000$$

GUESSTIMATE SUBTOTAL so far:
$$\$63,700 + \$6,370 + \$9,555 + \$2,548 + \$5,000 = \$87,173$$

Keep in mind that the average cost per square foot takes into consideration that rooms need material below it, above it, and to finish it out. It doesn't, however, include things like a new furnace to heat the addition. Also, as you can imagine, a bedroom with just sheetrock and a closet will cost less per square foot than a kitchen boasting granite tops and new cabinets. THIS IS ONLY THE FIRST ROUND OF BROAD-BRUSH-STROKE NUMBER GATHERING SO YOU CAN HAVE DISCUSSIONS ABOUT PRIORITIES BEFORE YOU CALL

Example 1

AN ARCHITECT. This is not a *guaranteed maximum price*. Have I said that enough times yet? Good.

STEP 4
Review Conclusions:

Congratulations! You made it through your first round of number crunching! It gets easier the more you do it. Soon you will be a professional cruncher, and able to sprint through options and ideas at lightning speed. Now that you have your $87k-and-change budget calculated, you and your partner will do one of three things:

1. Smile and realize that you might be able to add that bathroom you wanted! Figure out the area of an average bathroom (5'x9') and do the math again to determine if it all fits in your budget.

2. Frown and realize that you need to avoid including the kitchen in the addition.

3. Decide to move.

However, do you REALIZE what just happened?? You just saved thousands of dollars! Why?

MAIN POINT ALERT: DON'T MISS THIS: You have a means of giving an architect your priorities AND **you did it in a way that didn't require:**

☛ Paying your architect to draw up ideas, including schematic designs, plans, elevations, models, etc. on options you can't afford

☛ Losing loads of time getting drawings nailed down and waiting weeks (if not months) to get multiple bids from contractors

Example 1

82

✏ Waiting/paying to have your architect do another round of drawings that are more in line with your budget . . . once you determine what your budget is.

If the $87k is over your budget but you can afford the addition without the kitchen, you now have a means of specifying to an architect that you want only the laundry room and bedroom and that you were hoping to do it for, say, $50k–$65k (actual numbers are obviously up to you).

The ability to communicate that you don't believe you can afford a new kitchen will give the architect a lot of direction and keep her focused on the things that are most realistic and in line with your priorities. Alternately, you would have paid the architect to draw up the addition both with and without a new kitchen, fallen in love with the new kitchen, waited for pricing, and then found out you couldn't afford it. Why spend money on additional drawings if you don't have to?

Example 1

Example 2: Going Up

STEP 1:
Determine the areas you want to add

Suppose you want a master suite, an additional bedroom (and possibly a bathroom for the smaller bedroom), and a staircase. Let's break it down like we did in example one so it is in manageable pieces.

MASTER SUITE: The exact configurations are infinite so you can either break up the portions you know you want (do you want a walk-in closet, for example?), use the sample plans shown, search online, or check out my website www.waschastudios.com. I am going to use the example shown below and assume 303sf for the area. Feel free to manipulate the sizes of things to fit your needs. If you want a tub, for example, you could add a typical 6' x 3' tub to the area we are working with (add 18sf to 303sf). Don't worry about where it goes for now.

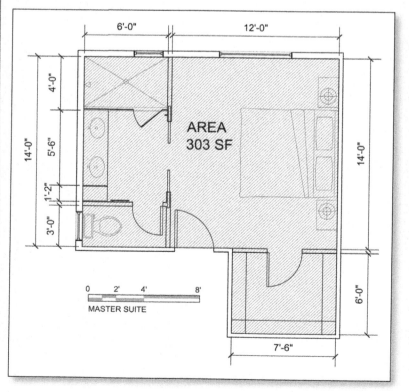

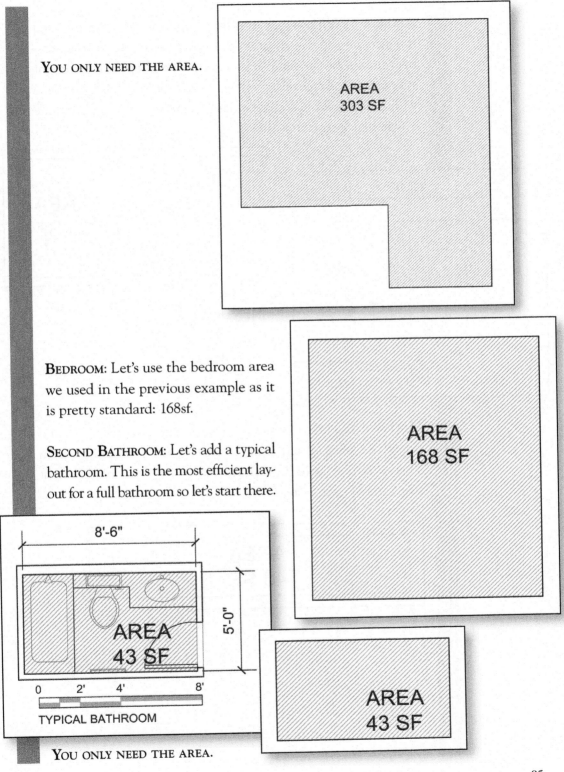

You only need the area.

AREA
303 SF

Bedroom: Let's use the bedroom area we used in the previous example as it is pretty standard: 168sf.

Second Bathroom: Let's add a typical bathroom. This is the most efficient layout for a full bathroom so let's start there.

AREA
168 SF

8'-6"

5'-0"

AREA
43 SF

0   2'   4'   8'

TYPICAL BATHROOM

AREA
43 SF

You only need the area.

STAIRCASE: What about a staircase? For now, you don't need to calculate the rise and run of an exact staircase to code. It is near impossible to determine if you will end up with a straight staircase, a switch-back, etc. If we go with standard sizes, a home with 8' or 9' ceilings and a standard stair width of 3' would require a switchback stair that is 69sf.

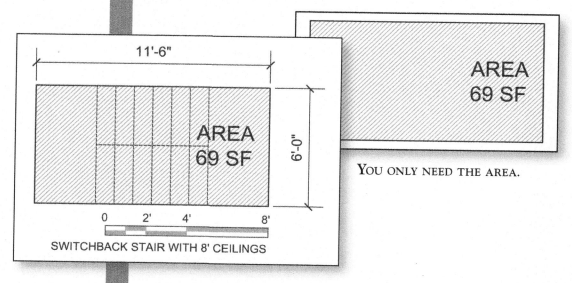

YOU ONLY NEED THE AREA.

SWITCHBACK STAIR WITH 8' CEILINGS

HALLWAY: You aren't going to get away with a second story and not have some sort of hallway, so let's use the 45sf example from the preceeding again. If you have a large second story you might need to add a bit more.

Example 2

STEP 2:

Determine the areas you are demolishing to add the new spaces

➥ Don't forget that when you add the area of a stair you need to multiply it by two because a 69sf staircase is affecting 69sf on the main floor and 69sf on the upper floor. If you are adding a new stair that goes from your basement up to the upper floor then you need to multiply the stair area by 3.

➥ If your goal is to try and use a main floor bedroom to add the stair, then go ahead and add the area of the entire room on the main floor along with the area of the new stair upstairs. For example, if you hope to use a 170sf bedroom on the main floor to add the stair, then add 170sf for the bedroom and 69sf for the new stair area upstairs.

➥ If you don't have any inclination about where you might want the stair that is normal. Go ahead and just multiply the stair size by the number of floors the stair is affecting. For our example we will multiply 69sf by 2.

All together we are adding:

$$303sf + 168sf + 43sf + 69sf + 69sf + 45sf = 697sf$$

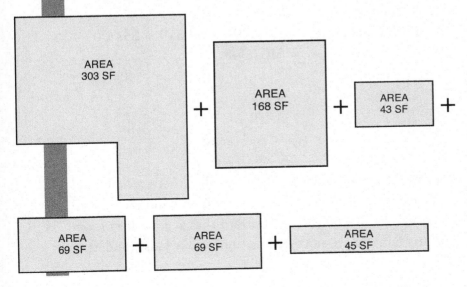

Do you see how I added 69sf twice? This is just a reminder that we added the space for the staircase on two floors. That always trips people up, so I thought I'd point it out again.

All together we are adding and demolishing 697sf:

$$697 \times \$175/sf = \$121,975$$

STEP 3
Now for the soft costs. . . .

ADD A 10-PERCENT CONTINGENCY:

$$\$121,975 \times 10\% = \$12,198$$

ADD 15 PERCENT FOR ARCHITECTURAL FEES:

$$\$121,975 \times 15\% = \$18,296$$

ADD 4 PERCENT FOR OTHER FEES:

$$\$121,975 \times 4\% = \$4,879$$

ADD SOME AMOUNT FOR RENT AND STORAGE:

$$\$5,000$$

GUESSTIMATE TOTAL PROJECT COST:

$$\$121,975 + \$12,198 + \$18,296 + \$4,879 + \$5,000$$
$$= \$162,348$$

STEP 4
Review Conclusions:

Nice work! You made it through example 2! Let's review. Add and subtract any rooms you are considering and recalculate as necessary. Maybe you can't afford that second bathroom upstairs but you are not psyched about your kids wandering

Example 2

into your bathroom from the adjacent bedroom in the middle of the night.

Then what's the point of a master bathroom if it isn't dedicated solely to the master bedroom you ask? Yes, that's a toughie. However, it isn't your job to solve this challenge. It is your job to determine what the challenges ARE and present them to your architect to solve. I'm not discouraging you from discussing what you might do about this bathroom challenge (or any challenge for that matter), but just understand that there will be factors you won't be aware of and solutions you likely wouldn't have come up with on your own. Discuss away, but know it isn't the end of the world if you can't figure out a solution you both agree on and love. Let the architect give it a whirl before you declare that the end of world has arrived . . . Or hang your partner by his or her toenails from the roof.

Just by doing these simple tasks you are multiple steps closer to your end goal, which is money in the bank. However, as I mentioned before, this cost-per-square-foot math doesn't include things like a new furnace, and obviously bathrooms are more expensive than bedrooms. If this broad-brush-stroke first step is making you batty, because you simply must have more accurate numbers in order to begin discussing your project, hang in there as I guarantee your architect will find this information immensely valuable. However, if your original assumption was that you could add a second story for half of what you just calculated, then you will be thrilled you did this exercise prior to paying for design drawings of something there is no way you can currently afford. Simply put, would around $160k for an addition make you choke, or would you say, "If we talk to an architect and the price can be within X percent of that number, we would be able to get a loan and do it"? Even this small bit of information gets you exponentially closer to having real conversations with your family or an architect than having had nothing at all.

Example 2

CHAPTER 10

NOW THAT YOU HAVE CRUNCHED SOME NUMBERS... WHAT'S NEXT?

W*hen beginning the interview process*, you will want to crunch any and all options you are contemplating before you meet with architects and contractors. Once you've discussed your ideas with them, you may need to modify your budget, your priorities, your image board, or all three. You will inevitably receive valuable feedback on your ideas, guesstimates, priorities, etc., so don't be discouraged if you have to make large changes to your plan. This is part of the learning process.

If your initial ideas don't work, or the architect suggests something that you love more, pregreasing your brain by crunching your own numbers ahead of time makes you better equipped to make decisions and weigh options.

- If the architect thought your ideas would work but increased the cost per square foot you were using, great. Get crunching.

- If the architect liked your plan but suggested a way to gain the extra space without screwing up your roofline (or other details you may not have considered), awesome. Revise and recalc.

✎ If the architect said you can't do the addition you wanted off the back of your house due to code issues or something else you weren't aware of, I am sure she will offer an alternate idea for you to start thinking about. You should be an expert by now if you need to crunch other ideas.

My main point is that regardless of whether you have to make large changes to your initial ideas due to the new information received from the architects and contractors you met with, the reason you were able to have such a detailed conversation in the first place was because you had real options and ideas to discuss. Would you rather have paid a few thousand dollars to get to this same point by not having done this exercise? That is what most people are forced to do because they don't have a way of comparing and contrasting things ahead of time. Congratulations, now you do!

DETERMINE WHERE THE IS MONEY COMING FROM

Before you proceed with hiring an architect, you need to determine where your money is coming from. Are you going to pay cash, call a bank, phone a friend, or buy a lotto ticket?

I am not in the business of advising people on their finances, but what I can tell you is that now is the point in the process when you want to be 100 percent sure you are able to obtain the money you need. This may seem obvious, but trust me on this one. I had a few clients who assumed they could get loans because of two (large) incomes in a single household but couldn't just because of the current regulations imposed by the banks. I had another client who couldn't get a loan despite his large income because all of his assets that banks would use as collateral were in his home country. You don't want to assume you can get the money you need for your project, go through the design process, and then find out the banks are being stingy. Paying your architect to redesign due to unforeseen surprises is exactly what we are trying to avoid.

The main thesis of this book is to properly prepare before you hire an architect, and skipping this step would be like not having picked up this book in the first place. Put the book down, and determine exactly where the money is coming from that will cover the total project cost including construction budget, contingency, architectural fees, other fees and even the vacation you decide you will need midproject.

SHOULD YOU PHASE YOUR CONSTRUCTION PROJECT?

What if you get to this point and realize you don't have a means of securing the money you need for the entire project to happen all at once? If you are contemplating phasing a construction project, you should plan on living in that house for at least ten-plus years to make the whole process worth it. Think about it. What has to happen in order to phase a construction project? It needs to be designed and broken out into pieces. You will most likely temporarily move, build, and move back in. After living there for a few years you will move, build, and reoccupy a second time.

If you don't think you will need a good three to five years between phases in order to save up the extra needed financing, then I recommend you seriously consider postponing the entire project until you can afford to do it in one go. Meaning if it will only take a year or so to save the additional money you need, then I highly recommend you not phase your project . . . just wait. Phasing a project is ultimately more expensive because you have to pay to remobilize everyone, and there are inevitably inefficiencies in getting your team's heads back in the game. There is also the cost and mental anguish associated with moving out. Just getting through a construction project is trying enough the first time . . . let alone twice.

If it is actually necessary to get you the home haven of your dreams, then by all means consider it. I just want you to be realistic about what qualifies as "necessary" and be aware of the pros and cons of phasing before you go for it. Phasing is a lot like a puzzle except that there is more than one way to put the pieces together. If done successfully, it can be a great way to get to what would normally be an unattainable goal by breaking up the process into smaller manageable pieces.

PHASING CONSISTS OF THREE MAIN STEPS:

1. Determine your LONG-TERM priorities: determining your priorities for phasing can sometimes be a bit different than determining priorities for a project you plan on completing all at once. If you are going to go through the process of breaking up your project into phases, you need to be darn sure your goals are all-encompassing. You would hate to complete phase 1 and realize that you should have enlarged the new kitchen to allow for future grandchildren. By all-encompassing, I really mean all-encompassing. Check out the list of questions about long-term priorities in Chapter 6.

2. Work with an architect to create a MASTER PLAN: all of your priorities and, ideally, all or most of your wish-list items, will be designed into one comprehensive Master Plan. We don't determine the design based on the phasing. Instead, we design everything just the way you want it and THEN figure out the best way to phase it.

   I recommend including more of your wish-list items than you may have otherwise been able to include in a non-phased project. It is an amazing feeling to be able to plan ahead for your long-term comfort and create a place you love to come home to. This mater plan will be the first time you see this longterm goal in a comprehensive manner. It's AWESOME! If you are going to bother stretching out the process and living there for the long haul, you might as well try for as many things as possible that will ultimately create your perfect home haven. You might not have originally planned on telling your architect about the outdoor kitchen you hoped to create when the project was long over, but I encourage you to literally include EVERYTHING to start. You can always cut things from the wish list later, but if your architect doesn't even know about it, she can't make suggestions like not locating the only operable window for the new second-floor nursery directly above the best location for the grill. Catch my drift?

3. Work with both your contractor and architect to nail down the best phasing strategy. Keep in mind that just because you have $200k to spend on phase one, and in five years you will have another $200k for phase two, doesn't mean that the most efficient use of your money is to spend all $200k in phase one. It might behoove you to spend only $100k upfront and wait to group certain things together in phase two when you spend the remaining $300k. Again, clarifying your priorities to your team will direct this process.

Don't be afraid to ask questions and think outside the box. Challenge your team to consider all variables that are important to you. Would you like to host a holiday party and need phase one to be completed by a certain date? Do you have family staying with you for the summer? Do you have severe allergies? Maybe you can group together certain air-contaminating tasks in phase one so you can live at home during phase two to save money. Sometimes these types of nonproject-specific issues that would not have otherwise made it into your list of construction priorities need to be taken into consideration.

Don't be afraid to voice anything and everything. Just ensure that everything is written down; there are so many variables specific to each project, and you want to make sure the whole team always has the updated list as you change and mold your project.

A COMMON PHASING MISTAKE YOU WANT TO AVOID

I want to point out a common mistake people make when phasing. I touched on it briefly in phasing step number two above, but I want to really engrave this on your brain with a hot branding iron. I once had clients who were initially interviewing architects to redesign their kitchen and bump out to create a large great room for their family. During the interview I casually asked them, "I realize you called me to talk about the main floor, but I want to make sure that you don't have some future project floating around in the back of your mind for the second floor. I ask because it can sometimes affect what we do on your main floor." They were, in fact, planning on remodeling their master suite at a later date (which happened to be located directly above the kitchen) but didn't mention it, thinking it had nothing to do with the main floor remodel.

I explained to them that if they try to move plumbing fixtures upstairs later, there would be a high likelihood they would need to rip open part of their new brand new kitchen ceiling to do it (or the new cabinets . . . depending on where the plumbing is located). Alternately, if they got stuck in a corner not wanting to rip open their new kitchen, they risked being very hindered with what they could change upstairs at a later date. They couldn't afford to do both projects at the same time, so I recommended that they allow me to design the master bathroom layout now with the rest of the main floor. I told them that if we know where the future plumbing fixtures and cabinets will be, we can install whatever plumbing and electrical might be needed for the future bathroom project while we have the main-floor walls opened up during this phase of construction. That way when they eventually demolished the master bathroom, all of the plumbing and wires would be right there in the necessary locations waiting for them to tie into. It only added a bit of extra cost to the initial design fees and saved them thousands of dollars in the long run.

Please, oh please, tell your architect if you plan on doing other projects later as your cash flow allows. Planning ahead for future remodels will inevitably save you money and heartache. If your projects end up having nothing to do with one another, great: nothing was lost by merely having that conversation. I'd rather not see you painfully destroy your shiny, new, sparkly remodel to access something you could have accessed before said remodel was finished.

PLAN AHEAD TO MINIMIZE YOUR STRESS

Phasing can be a challenging process, so don't forget that no question is a bad question. Also, keeping yourself excited about the end result will go a long way toward maintaining your sanity during the project(s). I highly recommend you keep your inspiration ideaspace readily available so you can refer to it, and remind yourself of the perfect home haven that awaits you. Don't underestimate the long-term strain of phasing but don't let it scare you away, either.

Think of ways you and your family might be able to rejuvenate between projects or midproject. Maybe you plan a vacation. Maybe you purchase a big gift certificate to your favorite restaurant ahead of time so when you are midproject and stressed out about money, you can enjoy an extravagant evening out without the associated stress of spending frivolously. Maybe you take an extra week off of work to move back in to ensure you have time to fully unpack. Don't spend three months living in your new remodel half unpacked because it will feel like you are still under construction. Your brain will inherently include that unsettled time as part of the previous construction process and make it that much more unappealing to begin phase two. Trust me, you won't be looking forward to it anyway, so don't add to the trepidation. Just bang out the unpacking. Most of all, don't forget that it will be AMAZING and totally worth it to have a home that feels like an oasis. Things will be larger, cleaner, less cluttered, or more functional—maybe all of the above.

SHARE BOTH YOUR GUESSTIMATES AND YOUR ASSUMPTIONS WITH YOUR ARCHITECT (ONCE YOU HAVE ONE)

The assumptions and guesstimates you are considering will get you moving in the right direction with your priorities, your architect, and ultimately your entire project. You must make careful notes during this process, as the validity of the assumptions associated with those guesstimates is as important as the priorities you determine as a result of them.

If the numbers indicate that adding on would be less expensive than going up and you decide to go that route as a result, make sure your architect is aware of your reasoning. Why? Let me give you an example. If the cost of concrete happens to be uncommonly high because of a run on some of the ingredients, the new concrete foundation (and resultant "less expensive" addition) could be falsely appealing. Your architect has no means of correcting this assumption if she doesn't know about it, so she would just proceed as directed when there could be better substitutions. You can see the difference between only telling your architect that you want an addition (giving her the impression that she shouldn't consider alternatives) and telling her you want an addition only because you assumed, based on the numbers you crunched, that it was less expensive than building a second story. Maybe you would also actually be okay with a second story if it turned out to be the better option.

By telling her everything, instead of just the end results, you are giving her an approximate budget (the numbers you crunched) and as much direction as you can possibly give her about your goals. That is all we ask. Providing her with a comprehensive list of your assumptions, likes, dislikes, goals, challenges, and priorities will ensure she starts as close to the finish line as possible and does not waste valuable time or money on things that you already know won't work for you.

CHAPTER 11

SELECTING YOUR TEAM: ARCHITECT, CONTRACTOR, OR ENGINEER... WHO DO YOU CALL FIRST?

THE SHORT ANSWER IS CALL THE ARCHITECT FIRST

The long answer is that regardless of what type of questions you are asking, you will save time by starting with the architect. Why? Let's look at a few common questions and see how they play out:

Example 1:

- ✏ HOMEOWNER'S QUESTION: "We want to add a second story, but we have no idea if our main floor and foundation can hold added weight. Do we need to call an engineer to ask about the structure, a contractor to ask about the price, or an architect to ask about the design?"

- ✏ ENGINEER'S RESPONSE: "Yes, you can add a second story. We might need to add a post or a new footing in a few places, but yes. Call an architect to figure out what you are doing, and then give me a call back."

Example 1

☞ CONTRACTOR'S RESPONSE: "Yes, you can add a second story. We might need to add a post or a new footing in a few places, but I would need to know what you want to do before I can give you any pricing information. You can count on $X dollars per square foot, but get with an architect to determine your design, and then we can talk about some numbers."

☞ ARCHITECT'S RESPONSE: "Yes, you can add a second story. We might need to add a post or a new footing in a few places to make it work. Given your goals, we could do X, Y, or Z. If you do some quick number crunching on those options, the price could vary. However, before you go down that road, you really should consider that your living spaces (kitchen, dining, living room) are already quite small for the number of bedrooms you currently have. If you add bedrooms upstairs, I really don't think you have the living space to accommodate the added people. Let's discuss in greater detail what your actual space requirements are before we spend lots of time on drawings and meetings with contractors and engineers."

Example 2:

Example 2

☞ HOMEOWNER'S QUESTION: "We want to add a mud room on to the back of the house and blow away the wall between the kitchen and dining room to open up the floor plan. Do we need to talk to an engineer first to see if this wall is load bearing, a contractor to tell us if we can afford it, or an architect to answer these questions AND provide design feedback?" (I know: that last one was a little loaded. But hey, I'm trying to make a point here.)

☞ ENGINEER'S RESPONSE: "Regardless of whether the wall is load bearing or not, you can open it up with a few minor changes. But there might be some code issues to be resolved before you can determine if you can add on to the back of the house.

I would just need to see what you want to do before I can provide any structural information."

↪ CONTRACTOR'S RESPONSE: As long as there are no code issues, we can make it work. You can count on this being about $X per square foot, but I would just need to see what you want to do before I can provide more accurate pricing information. Don't forget that we will need to add heating and cooling since your furnace is most likely not sized to handle the additional area."

↪ ARCHITECT'S RESPONSE: "Regardless of whether the wall is load bearing or not, you can open it up with a few minor changes. At first glance it appears that you can add on to the back of the house. However, if all you want is a mud room, we could potentially use the large walk-in closet in the guest bedroom for all or part of it to save money and not have to upgrade the furnace. If you went that route, you are probably looking at a ballpark figure of $X dollars. If we bumped out, you are probably looking at $Y dollars plus the cost of the heating and cooling. Let's figure out how much space you need in your mud room first, and we can go from there."

Architects don't just create designs. They can also assess your structure, provide pricing feedback, and offer insight regarding your priorities and goals. Don't get me wrong: I don't mean to imply that all engineers and contractors can't or won't offer suggestions and answer other questions. But they aren't trained (and don't get paid) to offer design advice, so when it comes down to it, they will suggest you call an architect before they can be of greater help.

HOW TO SELECT YOUR ARCHITECT

Selecting your team is one of the most important decisions you will make during the entire process, so if you are ever going to slack off, now is not the time to do it.

Things to think about when selecting an architect:

1. Determine if you are looking for a signature style.
   » Are you looking for someone who has a particular style that marks all of their projects? Some architects have a signature style and some don't.
   » Are you looking for someone whose portfolio indicates that he or she can work in multiple styles, is a creative problem solver, and can think outside the box?
   » If you get a stellar recommendation from a trusted friend for an architect who only does contemporary work but you have your heart set on a traditional white picket fence and house to match, she might not have the experience to design and detail things the way you want them. Don't be afraid to talk to her about this concern. Ask if she has done anything similar to what you want that might not be shown in her portfolio. Doing minimalistic projects is just as hard, if not harder, than those with a lot of ornate detail. All particular styles require someone who has experience in that architectural language. I don't recommend being a guinea pig even if the recommendation was awesome and you fall in love with the architect.

2. What type of services do you need, and do the architects you are considering provide those services?
   » Are you adept at reading architectural plans and, if not, can they provide alternate visual methods to help you understand them . . . like 3D models, for example? Maybe you need help understanding the process and are looking for someone, say, who has taken the time to write an amazing book in a way that is easily digestible by all, proving her ability to communicate ideas.
   » In addition to your architectural needs, do you need help selecting finishes, fixtures, furniture, art, etc., and do they provide those types of services? Some do and some

don't. If they don't, ask if they have a recommendation for someone they work well with.

» Do you want help managing the construction, or do you just need a set of permit drawings? If you only want permit drawings, is the architect okay with that? Make sure to ask her. Some prefer to be involved through to the end of the project to ensure the design intent is carried out.

3. If your project is of significant size, you should use a licensed architect. Designers cannot legally call themselves architects without actually having gone through the painstaking torture that is our licensing process. While I am sure there are qualified unlicensed designers out there, would you want a dentist that isn't board certified? No, thank you. Having a certified professional 100 percent in your corner during this challenging process is a huge benefit.

4. Call their references. Ask the architects you are interviewing if they have previous clients willing to let you visit their finished homes, and go do it. If not, make sure to call all of the references they provide. Ask those references about their experience with the architect, mention the services you need and see if they were provided any of the same. Also, always search for online reviews. Keep in mind that not all architects have an online presence, but that doesn't mean they are bad at architecture. It just means they are bad at marketing. Regardless, you should talk to real humans so you can ask specific questions about how well that particular architect listened, responded to challenges, managed the process, dealt with the schedule, determined the budget, etc.

5. What is their schedule? Do you want them to start right away? Can you get on their schedule for next summer if that works better for you? Don't just assume that because they took the interview that they can start immediately, and if it matters to you, ask.

6. Some architects charge for an initial interview and some
    don't. If you are serious about finding the right person, I
    wouldn't let this small initial fee influence your decision in
    any way. It takes about half of an entire work day to travel
    to a potential client's home, meet with them, travel back,
    and put together an estimate. This is time the architect can't
    spend on other billable projects. Afterward, you will inevitably
    be better educated about the process and maybe will have
    even snagged some ideas. Additionally, you will be perfectly
    prepared (after having read this splendid book) to discuss
    your list of priorities and project ideas for which you will get
    professional advice. There is value in that. Don't let a small
    fee put a damper on a potentially great working relationship.

7. Before your initial meeting, ask if you will be working with
    them personally or a project manager. You need to meet
    whomever you will be dealing with on a day to day basis. No
    one wants to be wooed by the tall, dark, and creative and
    end up working with the Grinch. Ask to meet the eventual
    team with whom you will eventually spend an inordinate
    amount of time (possibly for years to come)!

8. It is important to make sure your personalities match! They
    will need to get to know your preferences, daily routines,
    pet peeves, personal details, etc. Is this the type of person
    to whom you can see yourself divulging your obsessive
    compulsion to organize your laundry into lights, darks,
    whites, heavy fabrics, damp fabrics, and super soiled? Did
    you feel like she was listening well and answering your
    questions when you first met? Pay attention to your gut.
    If she doesn't seem like the right fit, on to the next one.
    Finding someone who matches your personality is just as
    important as her portfolio.

9. When you are interviewing architects make sure to share
    your priorities, the numbers you've been crunching, and the

list of assumptions you've been using to nail down those numbers and priorities. This is a priceless opportunity to learn a lot about the validity of the ideas you've been contemplating for some time now. It is also helpful to see how well the interviewees listen, respond, and their willingness to offer other ideas. This is a great time to test the waters, and it also gives the architect as much information as possible to provide an estimate that is on par with what you hope to achieve.

HOW MUCH DOES AN ARCHITECT COST?

That's a good question. Like most good questions, there is no one answer that fits every situation, so the answer is . . . it depends. Don't you love that? No? I touched on the average cost of architectural services in Chapter 8, but here is a bit more information to go by.

There are industry standards that most follow, but it is still contingent upon the circumstances. There is a difference in price depending on if your project is residential or commercial, what part of the country you live in, the size of your project, the level of experience of the architect, how much overhead a particular firm has, and so on. If you find yourself doing Internet searches, just keep all of that in mind. As always, it never hurts to pick up the phone and call a few to find out.

Architectural fees typically end up being a certain percentage of the construction cost. That percentage can be as low as 8 percent for less experienced firms or firms performing fewer tasks. You can expect to pay an average of 10 to 15 percent of the construction cost for most medium to large-sized projects, and 15 to 20 percent for high-end ventures or homes requiring a lot of custom details. Seem high? Trust me; it isn't. The extensive amount of properly detailed documentation will save you a lot of money in the long run.

WHAT EXACTLY DO THESE FEES GET YOU?

These percentages have been around for a while, and the services with which they are associated have also been a staple until recent changes in technology. The tasks associated with various phases of architectural services have historically been categorized like this:

- ✏ **10-PERCENT PRE-DESIGN:** This can include site analysis, code research, measuring your existing house, drafting your existing house, programming, goal setting, etc.

- ✏ **25-PERCENT SCHEMATIC DESIGN:** This includes designing options for your review, which could comprise plans, elevations, 3D models, renderings, or basically anything your architect needs to get her ideas across.

- ✏ **12-PERCENT DESIGN DEVELOPMENT:** This includes modifying the schematic design so there is enough information to get initial pricing feedback, and you are able to finalize the actual scope of work. From this point forward your architect will be working on one design concept headed toward final drawings.

- ✏ **35-PERCENT PERMIT AND CONTRACT DOCUMENTS:** This includes drafting the actual documents used to get your building permit, to finalize construction estimates, and to build from.

- ✏ **3-PERCENT BIDDING AND NEGOTIATING:** This includes helping owners navigate the estimates and contracts received by contractors.

- ✏ **15-PERCENT CONSTRUCTION ADMINISTRATION:** This includes any time spent on the project during construction answering questions, reviewing submittals from contractors and subcontractors, quality control, reviewing payment requests by the contractor, obtaining closeout documents, etc. This isn't always included in the estimates that you will receive from architects because it is extremely difficult to guess how many surprises will arise during construction. As a result, these percentages can vary; but this is a good starting point.

Keep in mind that there have been thick books written that describe in great detail what the various phases consist of. The phases, percentages, and tasks can change depending on the size of project, type of project (commercial or residential), and if the owner is willing to pay for every possible service available to them. The preceding list is based on commonalities typical of residential projects.

What the heck does all of this mean for your addition, you ask? It means that if your architect is charging you a total of $20k for her services that . . .

- $2,000 of it would for measuring and drawing existing conditions, reviewing codes, etc.

- $5,000 of it would be for designing.

- $2,400 of it would be for modifying the initial designs, and nailing down the final scope of work.

- $7,000 of it would be for doing the permit/construction drawings.

- $600 of it would be for reviewing the estimates and contracts that the contractors send you.

- $3,000 of it would be for doing various tasks during construction.

As I mentioned, you can find variations on a theme here. The advent of new technology, among other things, has begun changing these percentages around. For example, newfangled computer programs have begun front-loading the hours—in other words, more time spent designing and less time spent on permit documents. Also, in my experience clients want flexibility, so sometimes those percentages can vary for those reasons as well. This flexibility could allow them to select their own plumbing fixtures, for example. An architect would then pull that task out of her scope of work (and estimate), and the owners would do it themselves.

It also wouldn't be uncommon for a client to come to me with images, research on materials, or already have had someone out to see if their furnace can handle the addition. The ability to do research on the Internet has changed the game quite a bit. IN MY DAY we had to walk uphill both ways in the snow! When I started down my architectural path, computer drafting programs and the Internet didn't exist, which is a huge departure from where we are today.

Long story short, the work, fees, and estimates will forever be rapidly changing. Just be confident in the pieces of the puzzle that you need, and ensure you translate the architectural estimates from archi-babble into English so you can make educated decisions.

Back to what the heck this means for you . . . I wanted you to be aware of all this information because it wouldn't be uncommon for the architects you interview to describe their scope of work in those terms. However, when I have previously explained the above information to clients, all I've received in return was a blank stare. As a result, while I want you to *understand* the information, this is what I want you to *do*:

✏ Determine what services you need (design, permit drawings, finishes, etc.).

- ✆ Make sure all interviewees actually provide those services (ask before you bother meeting with them), and include those services in their estimates. The actual services you request might be hidden in the fancy groups of services noted above (like "Pre-Design" and "Design Development"). So make sure you ask what specifically is included and have them give that to you in writing so there is no confusion.

- ✆ Additionally, clarify in writing what is NOT included. For example, some architects contract directly with the structural engineer and some don't. This means the engineer's fees are included in the architect's fees. If that's the case, when you are determining your total project budget, you will know not to include the engineering fees a second time in those calculations. Knowing what isn't included will help you plan ahead for the total fees you should expect to pay during the process.

- ✆ Make sure you understand the estimates in their different forms to ensure you can compare the estimates apples to apples. Without knowing what is and is not included, one architect's estimate could seem quite inflated compared to another when, in fact, it isn't. Any good architect will expect you to be interviewing other architects, so there is no shame in asking them questions when you are trying to compare and contrast their estimates.

If you have questions, try this approach: "Hi there. I'm comparing a few different estimates, and yours doesn't spell out X, Y, and Z. Can you please verify if those are included?" If you hang up and later find yourself confused again, call back. Make sure to get answers for any and all questions before making your final decision about which architect to hire.

I wish there were a simple equation or check list I could give you but there isn't. You just need to pay attention, ask for explanations, and then evaluate the estimates based on the information you need. I realize part of that might seem self-evident, but sometimes it helps to hear that there is no one way to do things. If the estimates confuse you it is because they actually can be confusing. So don't think you are just missing some big piece to the puzzle. Have confidence in the fact that it is the professionals' job to explain things in a clear and understandable manner and educate you so you can make informed decisions. If you don't understand, ask more questions. Architecture is a foreign language in which you must become proficient.

WHAT TYPES OF ARCHITECTURAL ESTIMATES ARE THERE?

Now that you understand the meat and potatoes of the estimates, the various phases, and what might be included or excluded, we will jump into the various types of estimates. This is essentially the fee structure that defines how you will pay your architect, regardless of what is included or excluded. Common estimate types include:

- Fixed fee or "lump sum" for a fixed number of services

- Hourly fee for an undetermined set of services or partial services

- Percentage of the construction budget

Fixed Fee:

A fixed fee for a fixed number of services is pretty self-explanatory. You agree on the services and an estimate for those specific services before the architect starts. This works well for projects where the scope can be determined at the outset of the project. If you want a second-story addition of a particular size and defined number of bedrooms, you get an estimate specifying exactly what the architect plans to do and agree on it . . . now you've got yourself a fixed-fee contract. Don't forget that with that fixed-fee contract comes a fixed amount of services. If you decide midway through your project that your two-bedroom addition needs to be a four-bedroom addition, then you've just changed your portion of the agreement. If that happens, you should get a modified estimate (just as you got the first estimate) spelling out precisely what is included, what is not included, and what is left to do.

Hourly Fee:

I don't recommend going the hourly fee route. The process of building or remodeling a home is unfamiliar to homeowners and confusing to boot. There are many misunderstandings even if everything is spelled out in plain English, let alone if the scope is nebulous. Trust me. No one wins here. If you only require partial services for a small project, I would still recommend getting an estimate for those limited services instead of leaving it as an open-ended contract. There are always discrepancies among what an architect understands as necessary for a successful project, what an owner understands, what is expected, and what is subjective.

If you hire an architect to design a kitchen addition and agree to an hourly fee without clarifying the specifics, for example, you could end up paying both your architect and your cabinet maker to design your kitchen cabinets. The architect could be happily working away on her usual list of kitchen drawings, not aware of the scope limits in your head. When you receive her drawings and itemized invoice for the many hours spent on the cabinets, how do you gracefully get out of paying her for something you've already paid your cabinet maker for? You don't. Do I have to remind you of the corny breakdown of the word ASS-U-ME? I will anyway to make a point . . . assumptions make an *ass* out of *you* and *me*. Don't assume. Get everything in writing. Don't go with an hourly-based contract.

Keep in mind, it would not be uncommon for an estimate to be a combination of fixed and hourly fees. Anything that the architect can determine with reasonable accuracy could be the fixed portion of the estimate. This could include pre-design items (like measuring, site analysis, etc.), permit/contract documents, and the like. Architects should be able to call on previous experience to make educated guesses about how long it will take them to complete certain non-nebulous tasks.

Examples of things that are more difficult to quantify are the number of client meetings, the number of times you will change your mind, and how many surprises there will be during construction. Every architect might do things a little bit differently but should gladly be willing to explain what's what.

In some estimates an architect might list out all of the services needed for residential design because from time to time they might not end up doing a few of them. As previously mentioned, a homeowner could end up picking his or her own light fixtures, for example. If that is a particular line item in an estimate, then you know exactly how much to subtract from the total if it is removed from the architect's scope of work.

A colleague of mine prefers to go the broad-brush-stroke route of capping her fees at a certain percentage of construction without breaking down all of the particular services. She bills hourly for whatever work is complete but also gives you the option of doing some of the work yourself. If you compare the two estimates, they could both ultimately cost the same amount, be for the same amount of work, and offer a similar level of a la carte flexibility, but one happens to be spelled out more than the other. Again, there is nothing wrong with asking for clarifications on anything you aren't able to parcel out yourself.

Percentage-based Fee:
Using a percentage-based fee structure is a common and completely acceptable route if you are unsure of what the ultimate scope of your project will be. You will see this often when homeowners want to have a few wish-list scenarios priced out. For

example, if you are unsure if you will include building a pool house with the renovation of your French Chateau, the budget could vary wildly between options. More house equals more drawings. More drawings equal more fees. Fair enough? The fees need to be proportionate to the work being asked of the architect, but if you don't know if the project budget will be $350k or $550k there is no one fixed estimate that will cover both.

THE REASON WHY ARCHITECTURAL DRAWINGS ARE IMPORTANT

Everyone claims that construction projects always go over budget. The thing is, construction budgets don't just magically grow like bean stalks for no reason. Simply put, you go over budget when there isn't a sufficient contingency, the drawings were not detailed enough, or both. Believe it or not, the cost could have been visible at the beginning of the project. However, everyone wants to hear that they can get what they want for the budget they happen to have available.

Contractors want to make clients happy (they are human like the rest of us). They try to determine a way to get their clients *a version* of what they want for the budget they have on hand. As a result, the contractor will make some assumptions and crunch some numbers to determine the least expensive way to get the project to work within the given budget. The problem, however, is that it is impossible for any contractor (or anyone for that matter) to write down every assumption that will ultimately create his or her *version* of the project.

The disconnect happens when contractors reveal some of his or her cost-cutting measures (like the inclusion of a simple faucet instead of the fancy one you had your eye on because it wasn't specified one way or the other in the drawings). If the clients don't happen to like the newly discovered inclusion, they change it.

That, my friend, is the definition of a change order.

Multiply this by one hundred and, voilà, we are now over budget. How do you avoid this? Pay your architect to include as much information as possible in the drawings to avoid situations where the contractor is making assumptions, and include an adequate contingency for surprises.

I know what you are thinking. You are thinking, "Didn't she just say that no human can possibly get every detail down on paper? If everything can't possibly be included, what should be included?" YOUR PRIORITIES. (Are you seeing a theme here?) If the entire team is clear about what your priorities are, then any assumptions that do have to be made can be made within those parameters. If you elect not to pay an architect to provide that kind of detail, then you need to increase the contingency so you have the budget available to pay for surprises. Either way, if you decide you want a fancy faucet over the place holder the contractor selected, you will have to pay for it regardless of whether you knew about it ahead of time or not. If you are lucky, the change order for the upgraded faucet will only cost you the difference between the price of the two faucets (and the restocking fee). If you are unlucky, it might require that you change the sink, vanity, backsplash height, or other similarly related items to get it to work. The key is knowing in advance, so you can plan your finances accordingly.

If you are forced to pay for five or six of these surprises at the beginning of the project and ultimately use up your contingency, the next three or four that arise will compete with your priorities. You might have to give up your awesome hot tub to avoid having a heat duct in a crappy location. See what I mean? You get what you pay for one way or another.

Knowing as much as possible ahead of time will allow you to freely pick and choose between various options . . . instead of wishing you had known what you know now way back when. Hindsight is 20/20. Or rather, architectural drawings are 20/20.

Ultimately, a successful project is not feeling like you were forced to compromise your priorities. When the construction is complete and the contractors are long gone, no one wants to see something every day that they wish they would have done differently. The higher your contingency and the better your drawings, the less of these compromises there will be. Both give you the ability to choose between what you want and don't want. Don't give that up before the project even starts.

YOUR RELATIONSHIP WITH YOUR ARCHITECT SHOULD BE BASED ON TRUST

Speaking of horror stories about projects going over budget, some believe that it behooves them to camouflage their actual financial cap and tell their architect that their maximum budget is less than it really is. Let me explain why this doesn't benefit you.

Picture yourself getting through months of design decisions and a massive amount of detailed drawings for the permit set. Concrete is poured, framing is finished and the electricians and mechanical contractors got through their inspections. The sheetrock got its final sanding, the cabinets and tiles are ordered, and you suddenly have a magnificent realization! You realize that you are pretty close to your chameleon budget because the rot the contractor found in the wall was fixed and paid for out of your contingency, and the drawings beautifully depicted your priorities to avoid unnecessary changes. Now you think to yourself, "I can afford to buy that wonderful soaking tub I've always wanted! Good thing I didn't divulge my real budget!" Not so fast . . . What would have been a $2,000 tub just quadrupled in cost, because in order to get it to fit, the toilet needs to move over one foot, which means the waste line running down to the basement and the vent running up through the roof need to move, which moves the new studs that are supporting the new sheetrock, which houses the new electrical wires behind the new cabinet. Get my drift? What should have happened was you should have given your architect your wish list and actual budget and worked together to fit as many of them into the project as possible from the very beginning. I can't stress enough how important it is to have all of your priorities in order, plan for a contingency, and be honest with your architect about your financial cap.

HOW TO SELECT YOUR CONTRACTOR

A good contractor is worth his or her weight in gold. It takes years of experience and a creative yet pragmatic thinker to foresee challenges and act accordingly while carefully considering the many trades and details involved. I have the utmost respect for good contractors and enjoy working with them. When selecting a contractor, you should call around and chat briefly with as many as you can to get a feel for their personality and the world in which you are about to enter. I'm sure you've found some random articles online like, "The Five Questions You Need to Ask Contractors" or "The Three Things You Need to Look Out for When Selecting a Contractor." If not, you should go find some. There are millions of them, and many of them are helpful. I want to focus on something else here, though.

There is a wide range of contractors who will provide you with a lovely array of estimates for the same amount of work, and you need to know how to make sense of it all. Take a step back and look at the big picture. You have your low, medium, and high-priced contractors to choose from. You need to begin by asking yourself what level of service you are expecting. If you want super-creative, unique, custom details, built with the highest level of craftsmanship, don't expect the low- to medium-priced contractors to do it. Maybe many of them could, if given unlimited time and budget, but their low- or medium-priced estimate indicates that isn't what they are planning for your project.

It also is a good indication that low or medium-priced work is their standard modus operandi. If you are just looking for a straightforward and comfortable home requiring less specialized talents, then maybe you do want to work with a contractor who costs less. But consider the following: Most contractors purchase their materials from the same places and use similar subcontractors who, in order to be competitive, need to charge competitive (i.e., similar) rates. As a result, many times the reason Contractor A's estimate is so much lower than Contractor B's and C's isn't because they have the inside track on super cheap labor and materials that will magically get you the same high-quality end result, right? And even if they did, my guess is they would still charge you the going rate and keep the profit for themselves.

Taking all of that into consideration, it becomes clear that your project is going to cost a certain price regardless of who does it. The difference is whether you will know about the additional costs ahead of time (in a detailed estimate) or after the fact (via change orders). I am not implying that low-cost contractors are being dishonest. They are human. Everyone likes to tell people what they want to hear, and everyone likes to make a profit. They are just used to a certain level of detail, and it is your job to determine if that level of detail is for you.

If you are a person who likes numbers, one of the only black-and-white figures you can easily compare is how much each contractor marks up his or her products and services. I've seen percentages ranging from 10 to 20 percent, and you can typically find this number clearly spelled out at the end of the estimate. Outside of that, the demo still needs to be hauled away, the finishes still need to be added, and the building still needs to be enclosed. If one bid includes demo but doesn't include the hauling and dump fees (creating a visibly cheaper estimate), do you think that the contractor is just going to generously flip the bill for that out of his or her own good will? No, you will. Surprise! Don't select your contractor based on who has the lowest bid, as many times all that it means is that his or her estimate is lacking things the other contractors have included that you will have to pay for one way or another. Contemplate these ideas instead:

- ☞ Talk to him or her about your priorities, the numbers you have been crunching, and the associated assumptions. See how he or she responds and how helpful he or she is.

- ☞ Ask yourself if you felt like your concerns were being heard during your meeting.

- ☞ How responsive are they?

- ☞ CHECK REFERENCES! I hope I don't have to beat this key point to death for you to understand how incredibly important it is.

- ☞ When you finally get estimates, ask yourself if they were easy to absorb and understand. Why is this important? This is what your invoices are going to look like. Does he or she act defensive when you ask questions about it?

- ☞ Although I recommend initially chatting with many contractors, I would only ask two or three for estimates. Any good contractor will take a lot of time to put together a detailed estimate, and any more than three, in my opinion, isn't necessary to get an accurate feel for the cost of your project. Respect their time and give them a fair shot at being awarded the contract.

HOW TO BE A GOOD CLIENT

Another important thing to consider when you are trying to find a contractor is that you want him or her to want to work with you as much as you want to work with them. I'm going to give you a few things to consider that will make you a desirable client.

Picture yourself as a contractor who gets a call from a potential client, who explains that they wanted to talk with you to get pricing information before they bothered calling an architect. You ask, "Pricing on what exactly?" The homeowner then launches into the various projects that they've been tossing around, and you patiently listen because you understand how overwhelming it can be to have a myriad of ideas with no real information about process or price. Sometime later, you leave your current (paying) job site to see the house in person and meet with the homeowners. They explain that they might be able to come up with more money if the price is right, but they need to know what things cost before they can make any determinations.

You immediately recognize numerous challenges surrounding their ideas and budget, given the existing conditions you observe. Nothing is impossible, but you need more information and clarity to proceed properly. You see that each of their ideas leads to several different options for which you couldn't responsibly give them pricing without having more to go on . . . even if they are only requesting "Off the cuff" or "We won't hold you to it" numbers.

You give them a cautious appraisal of the various challenges connected to one or two of their ideas, while trying to avoid unnecessarily scaring them off. They sit and listen with that deer-in-headlights look, and you ultimately suggest that they call an architect to help determine a design that can properly be priced out. And that is just ACT 1.

ACT 2 begins months later once an architect is finally involved, and in comes the first round of drawings to be priced out. You commence the multiple-week process of calling on trusted subcontractors, touring them through the house to get accurate pricing, and combining their numbers with yours. You get clarifications, calculate material quantities of everything from sheetrock to roofing, create spreadsheets to see how the timing would work out with your other projects, and compile the huge amount of information into something cohesive.

Once you receive the call that the price is too high, you play the waiting game (for who knows how long) until the second (and many times third) round of drawings arrive. You then sheepishly request new information from your subs for which neither you nor they are being paid . . . or paid enough. All the while you are well aware that industry standards would have one, and sometimes two other contractors, competing for this same exact project.

Well, on behalf of architects and homeowners everywhere, I'd like to personally thank you for all of the many hours you've helped move budgets around. It is an invaluable service, but one I'm sure you wish you charged for (or charged more for).

Now let's go back to you being the homeowner. All contractors knew what they were getting into when they got into this business. You win some and you lose some. The kicker is, by you opting to start the process without any good sense of your priorities or budget, you are potentially sending many contractors (and sub-contractors) through many rounds of pricing unnecessarily . . . and only one of them will get the job.

I want to share with you a few rules of thumb that I tell all of my clients (or anyone contemplating working with a contractor). The first, as mentioned earlier, is that you only want to request initial pricing from two to three different contractors. If I was a contractor and I knew that five different companies were estimating this job, I would decline just because the chances of getting the job at that point don't outweigh the time it will take to put the pricing together in the first place. The second bit of advice is to not request pricing on design you already know isn't quite flushed out. If you don't know if you can afford your addition and need the pricing in order to continue making decisions, that's great. Go for it. If you already know that you need to add a bedroom to the design to make it even remotely feasible, don't ask for pricing on an earlier (inaccurate) design just to see where you are at fiscally, knowing things will change. Be a good steward and a good client and contractors will flock to you. Everyone wants their time and energy to be respected and contractors are no exception. They are a key member of the team, and a great team is the best way to a successful project.

IF YOU ARE CONTEMPLATING A DESIGN-BUILD COMPANY, CONSIDER THIS

I'm sure you've heard of the age-old conflict between architect and contractor. They're not supposed to get along, stereotypically. But today's society is moving toward interdisciplinary occupations, and people are getting increasingly better at working together, gradually alleviating this conflict. More design/build companies (where the contractors and architects are both working for the same company) have begun to emerge.

Not all of the perceived benefits are actually beneficial, however. One common claim made by design/build companies is that architects don't know how to build and having in-house contractors alleviates the many issues that arise as a result.

To offer an obvious rebuttal, you can't paint the entire architectural profession with a broad brush stroke. Do I need to remind you to select an architect with actual experience? No? Good. Next, if you were to momentarily entertain the notion that architects don't know how things go together, the claim that contractors are coming to the rescue would be the case regardless of whether the two occupations are part of one company or separate companies. Both architects and contractors are central to the process, but do they really need to be under one roof?

I've known both architects and contractors who've owned design/build companies and eventually went back to their respective corners. WHY? They couldn't do both the architecture and construction well AND be profitable all at the same time. Key point here—paying attention?— the fact is, in our rapidly changing world, it is difficult enough to be good at one type of business, let alone two. When you have the added burden of concerning yourself with both occupations AND being profitable, the *client* will always lose. It can be an inherent conflict of interest. Part of our duty as your architect is to protect your interests. We are your advocate and produce a contract set of documents (your construction drawings are actually appropriately called "contract documents") to depict your wishes. This reflects an agreement between you and your contractor and is used to set a price for the cost of construction. If the person writing your contract and the person executing it are under one roof, it would be like allowing your insurance company to determine which medicine you take . . . Oh wait, they do. I love that. Don't you?

CHOOSE YOUR TEAM WISELY

As I have said before, you will ultimately spend a huge amount of time with your team, and many times for multiple years to come. For example, I am currently working on a project where I first met the couple before they decided to have children. Now we are midway through construction and their second son is two years old. I had a contractor comment to me once, half-jokingly, that he sees our client more often than his own spouse. When you begin your search for your team you must go into it knowing it is like a long-term partnership. You don't have to argue about who is going to take the garbage out, but you are creating your home together. These are important decisions as these are important relationships. Choose wisely, young grasshopper.

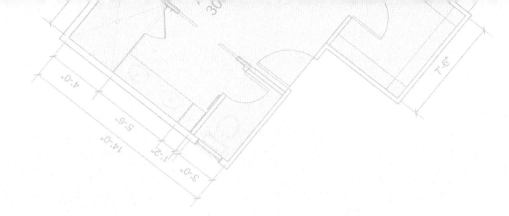

Dear Homeowner,

You now have tools to help you navigate your way through a challenging, yet immensely rewarding remodel. Honestly, that is awesome! Not everyone has the fortitude to actually go for it, but you do! Congratulations!

It doesn't have to be as hard as people make it out to be. It won't ever be easy, but with this guide it will be vastly easier. Things may seem scary when there are unknowns associated with them. We all have turned unfamiliar tasks into whirling tsunamis of horrifying madness just because our lack of experience disallowed us to organize them into pretty, little compartments with ribbons on top. I know I have!

I realize people in most professions essentially keep a "professional" distance from their clients. They stick to the business at hand and steer clear of the emotions attached. However, architecture is a super-personal business. At least, it is for me anyway. You tell me your hopes and dreams, I learn about your pet peeves and fears, and I consistently observe the oh so common elements that cause emotional charge between family members. I simply have to breach that professional barrier, and offer some advice on both the logistical and emotional elements associated with taking on a remodel. Use this book however it serves you best. Just have confidence in knowing that the contents are directly siphoned from hundreds of homeowners just like you. You aren't alone.

Last, but definitely not least, know that your efforts will result in a fantastic oasis that you and your family will fall in love with. I'm not just talking about a light, bright, organized, structure of awesomeness. I'm talking about a home that, if desired, can be in your family for generations. A space in which, when you enter, you siiigggggghhhhh an elongated sigh and think, "Finally, I'm home."

Sincerely,

Stephanie

ABOUT THE AUTHOR

Have you ever created something (a product, piece of art, or great meal for example) and felt an enormous sense of satisfaction watching the end-user enjoying or benefiting from it in some way? That satisfaction is what drove Stephanie Wascha to become an architect, write her blog, and ultimately become the author of Dear Homeowner, Please Take My Advice, Sincerely, An Architect. Stephanie is a licensed architect with over 18 years of residential experience and runs her own architectural design firm, Wascha Studios, in Seattle, Washington. The positive reader response and homeowners' overwhelming need for helpful information when commencing with any kind of home modification, lead her to create an online consulting business to help people everywhere properly prepare for their next big project.

www.waschastudios.com

CPSIA information can be obtained
at www.ICGtesting.com
Printed in the USA
BVOW10s1104030118
504353BV00024B/1298/P

9 780998 117607